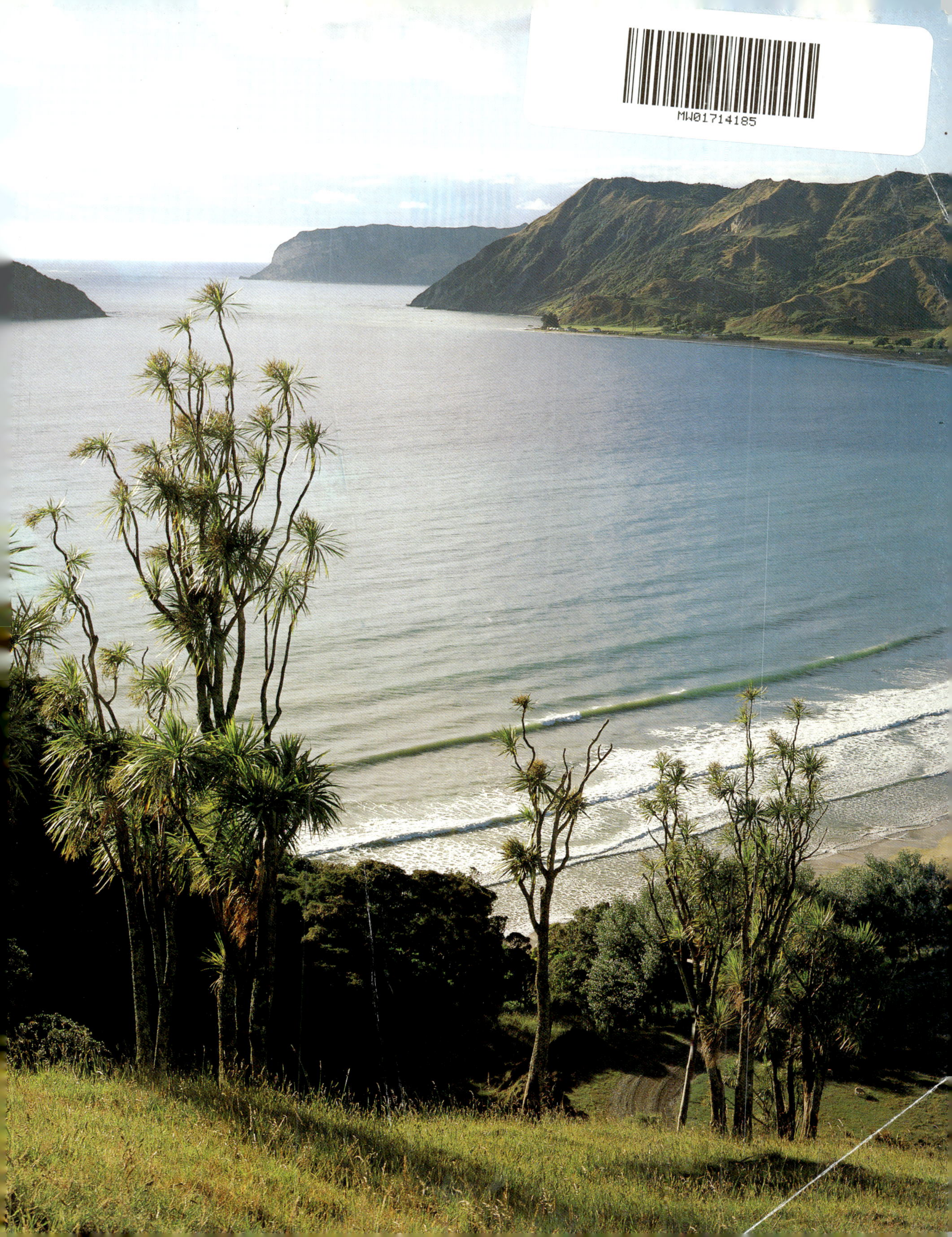

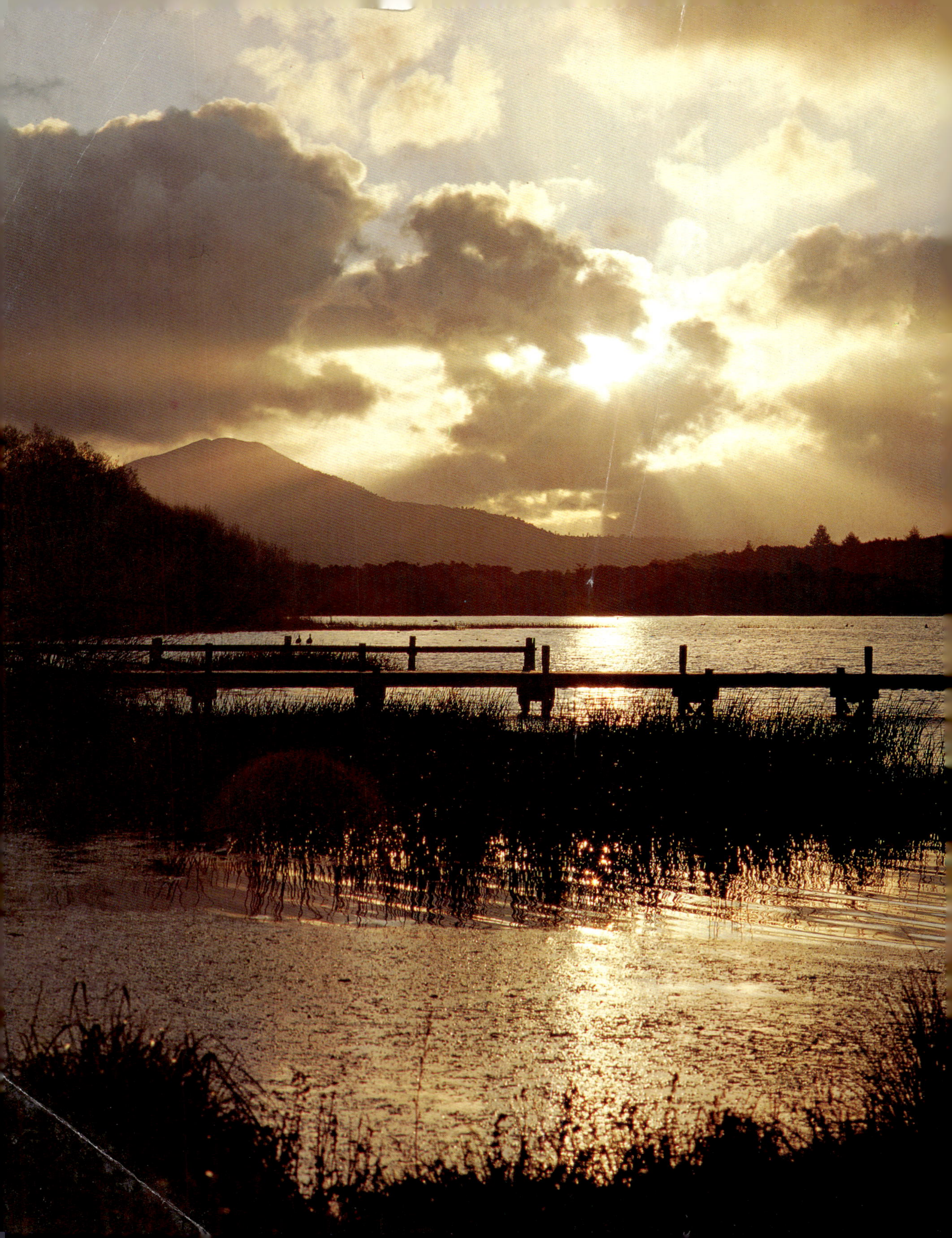

Pictorial New Zealand

Photography by
Warren Jacobs
Text by
Errol Brathwaite

KOWHAI

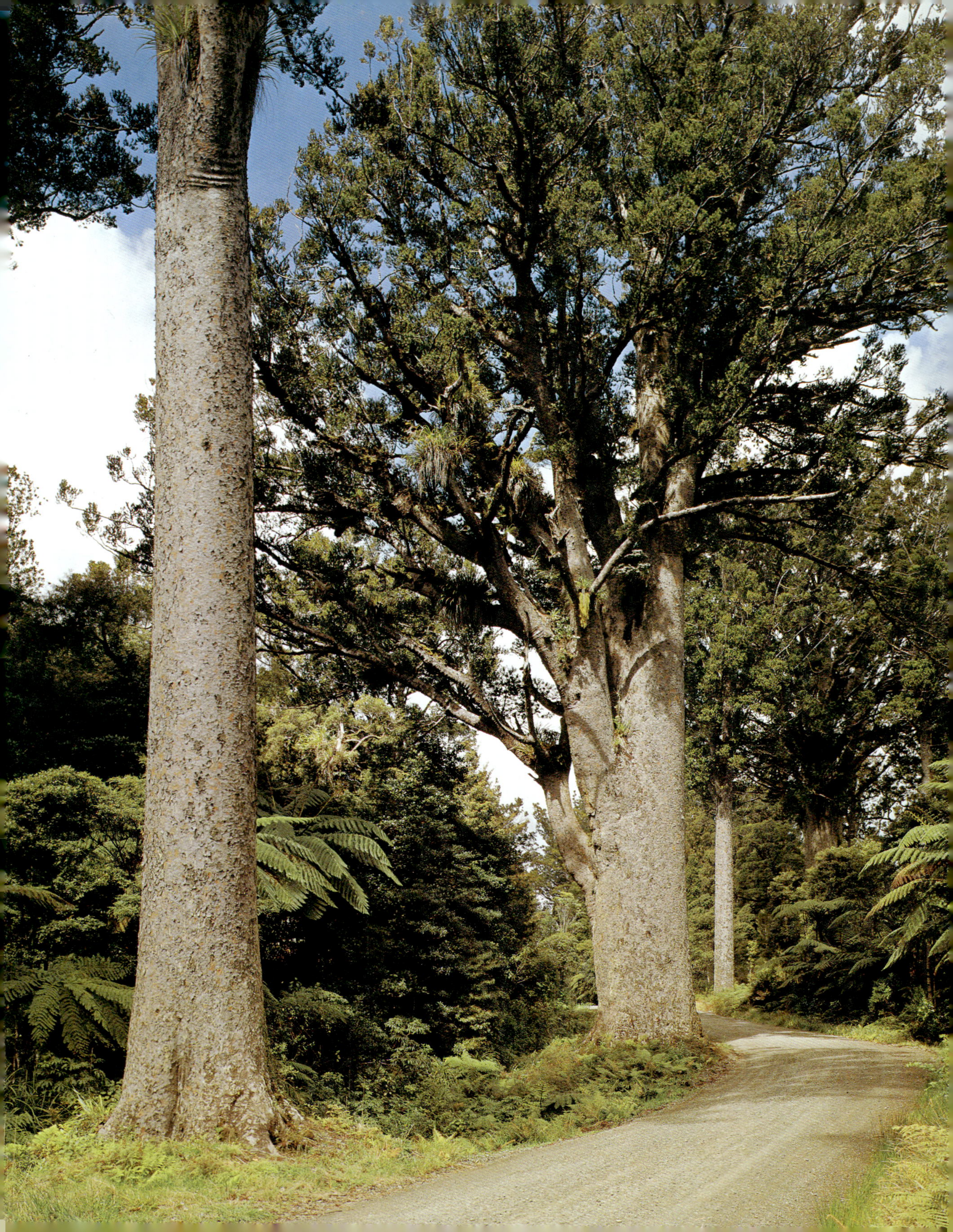

Introduction

New Zealand is a painter's or a photographer's dream of a country. The climate, though it displays an astonishing variation over so small a land area, is universally kind enough to present frequent and long days of excellent visibility; and because of the islands' long and narrow shape, the clear ocean light ensures almost studio-perfect conditions.

The scenic quality of New Zealand's landscapes is superb, offering within a land area of a mere 10,000 square miles ranges of gleaming mountain peaks over 3,000m high, active volcanoes, lakes of vast area and awesome depth; fjords whose mountain walls rise 1,500m sheer and vertical from the cold sea; rivers hundreds of miles long, some navigable for much of their length, often confined within dark, deep gorges, sometimes spilling across plains as tangled strands of gravel-choked waterways.

There are tamed and tidy areas which are domains of hedged and tree-shaded husbandry, there are wild mountain valleys brown with tussock and snowgrass, and there are deserts of sour pumice soil supporting a fantastic variety of flora.

The seascapes range from rock-bound coasts as storm-battered and unyielding as those of Cornwall or Maine — and golden curves of ocean beach backed by forest and protected by bush-crowned headlands, olive-drab foliage splashed in season with scarlet pohutukawa, or presided over by nikau palms and washed by a dazzling white surf, fringe of a deep blue sea.

The variety includes one mountain of over 3,600m, sixteen of over 3,048m, thirty-two of over 2,743m and one hundred and fifty-seven over 2,134m high.

The longest river is the Waikato, in the North Island — 270 miles of strongly flowing, deep, not to say fierce river, navigable for small craft in its lower reaches. The largest river, (though not the longest), is the South Island's Clutha, discharging over two million cubic feet of water into the Pacific Ocean every minute. The most navigable river is the Wanganui, flowing out where the North Island's west coast swings out in a long thrust into the Tasman Sea. Until comparatively recent times, it carried passengers and freight to Taumaranui, a port in the central highlands of the island!

New Zealand's more than 4,000 miles of coastline is deeply indented, forming many fine, sheltered harbours, the finest of which occur where the coastline cuts across the directional trend of the high ranges. These are seldom important commercially, however, being walled by steep mountainsides and separated from population centres by vast ranges of very high mountains. The most important harbours are in drowned river valleys, (Auckland and Wellington), the drowned crater of an extinct volcano, (Lyttelton), and a narrow strait between a volcanic island and the shore, one end of which has been blocked by an upheaval of land, (Dunedin.)

This, of course, is typically New Zealand. It is, above all, a land of contrasts and contradictions. There are cities sprawling cheek-by-jowl to form urban populations of up to half a million; and cities sitting in the midst of pastoral areas, which, with populations of hundreds of thousands, have contrived to remain big small-towns, in their layout and their character.

There are sudden, green, fruitful valleys in the midst of a sun- and frost-blasted landscape where the summers bring burning heat and the winters iron-hard frosts and snow; harbours that would shelter a large navy, visited only by occasional fishing vessels and pleasure-craft — and harbours

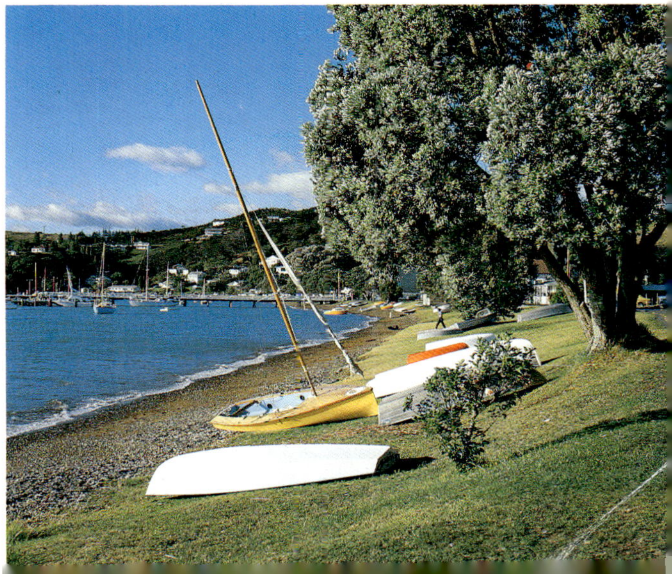

The Kauri tree, once milled almost to extinction, (they take a thousand or more years to mature), is protected in Waipoua State Forest . . . . and Kororareka, once busy with whaling ships, is now the haunt of pleasure yachts and launches, and is known as Russell.

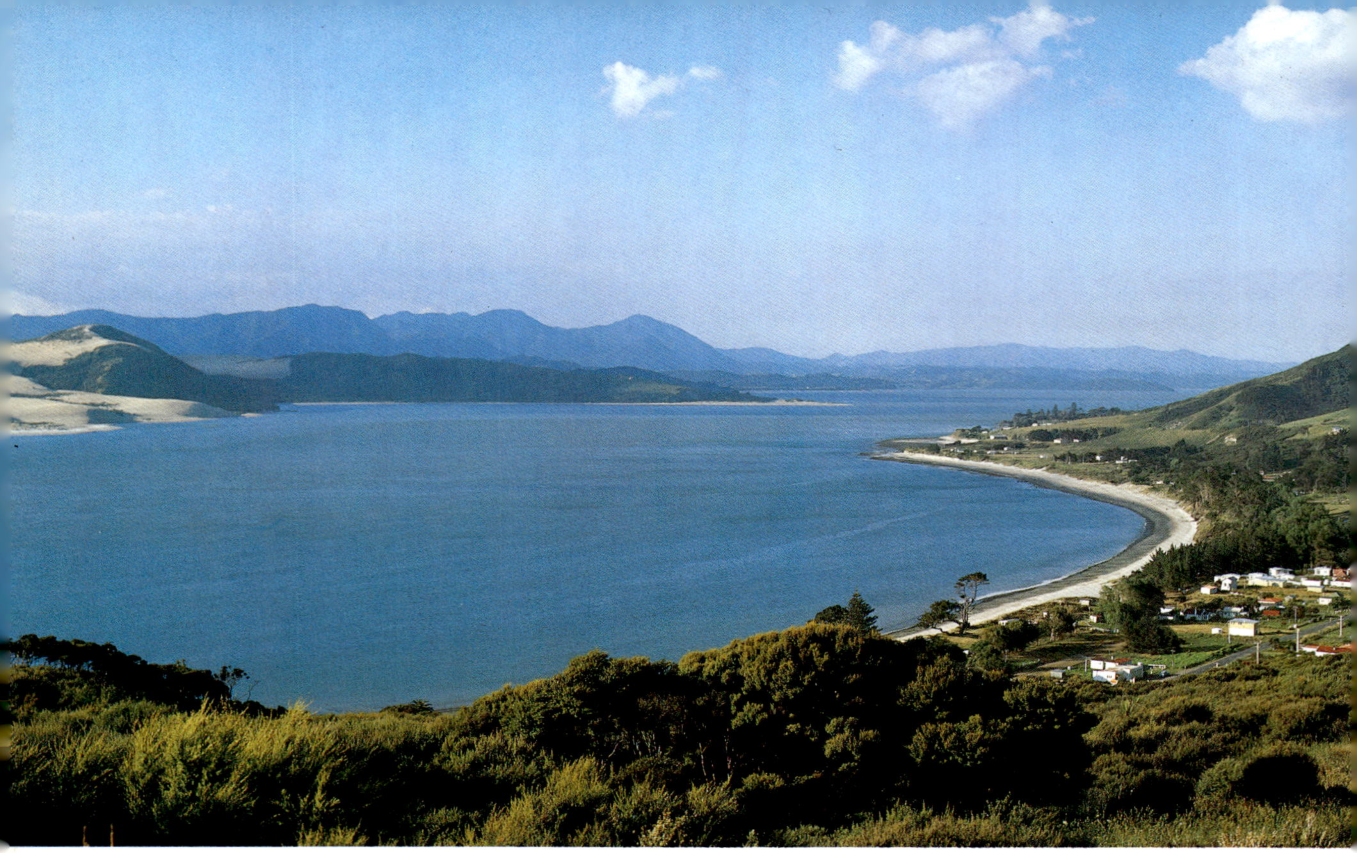

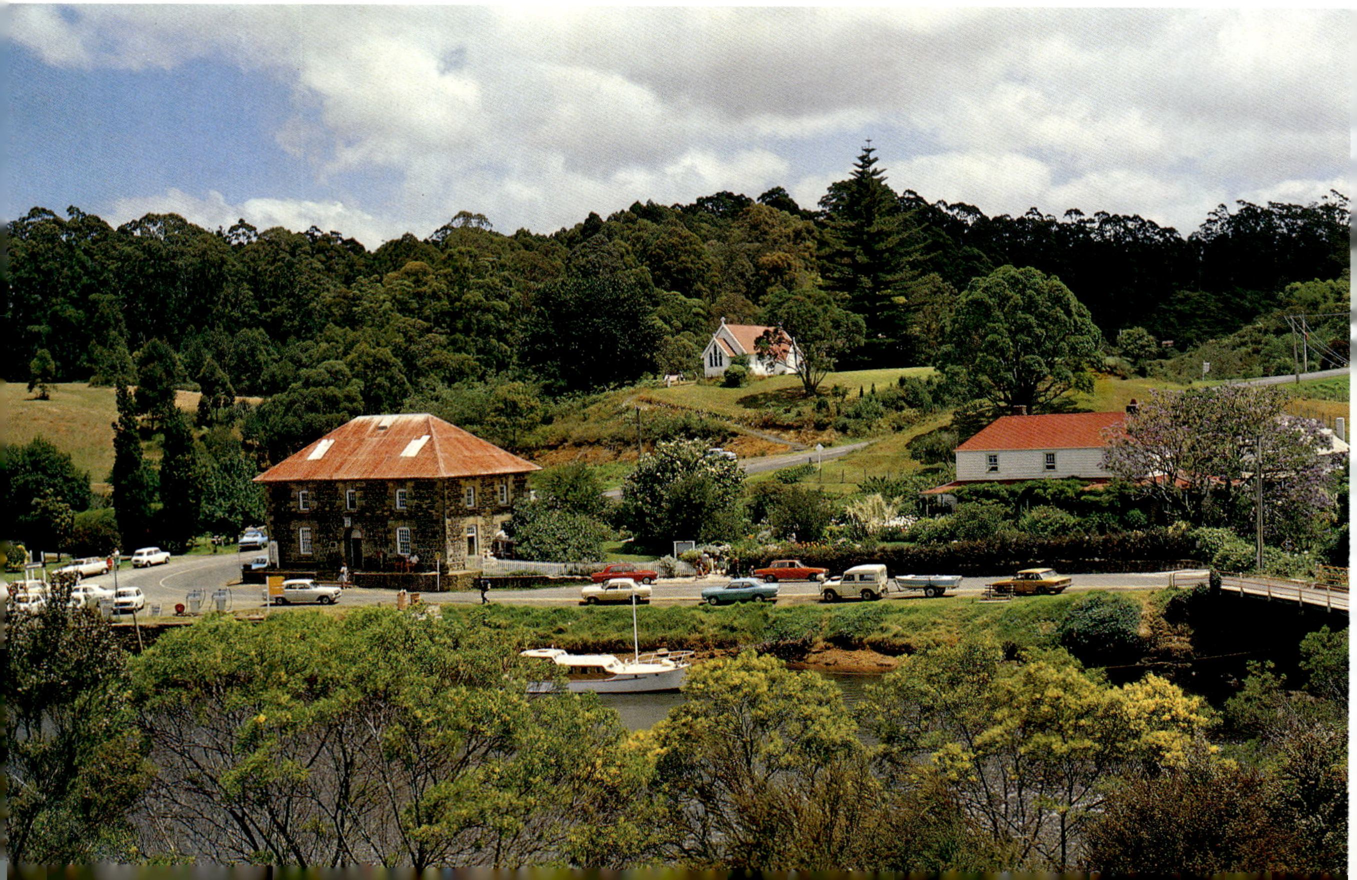

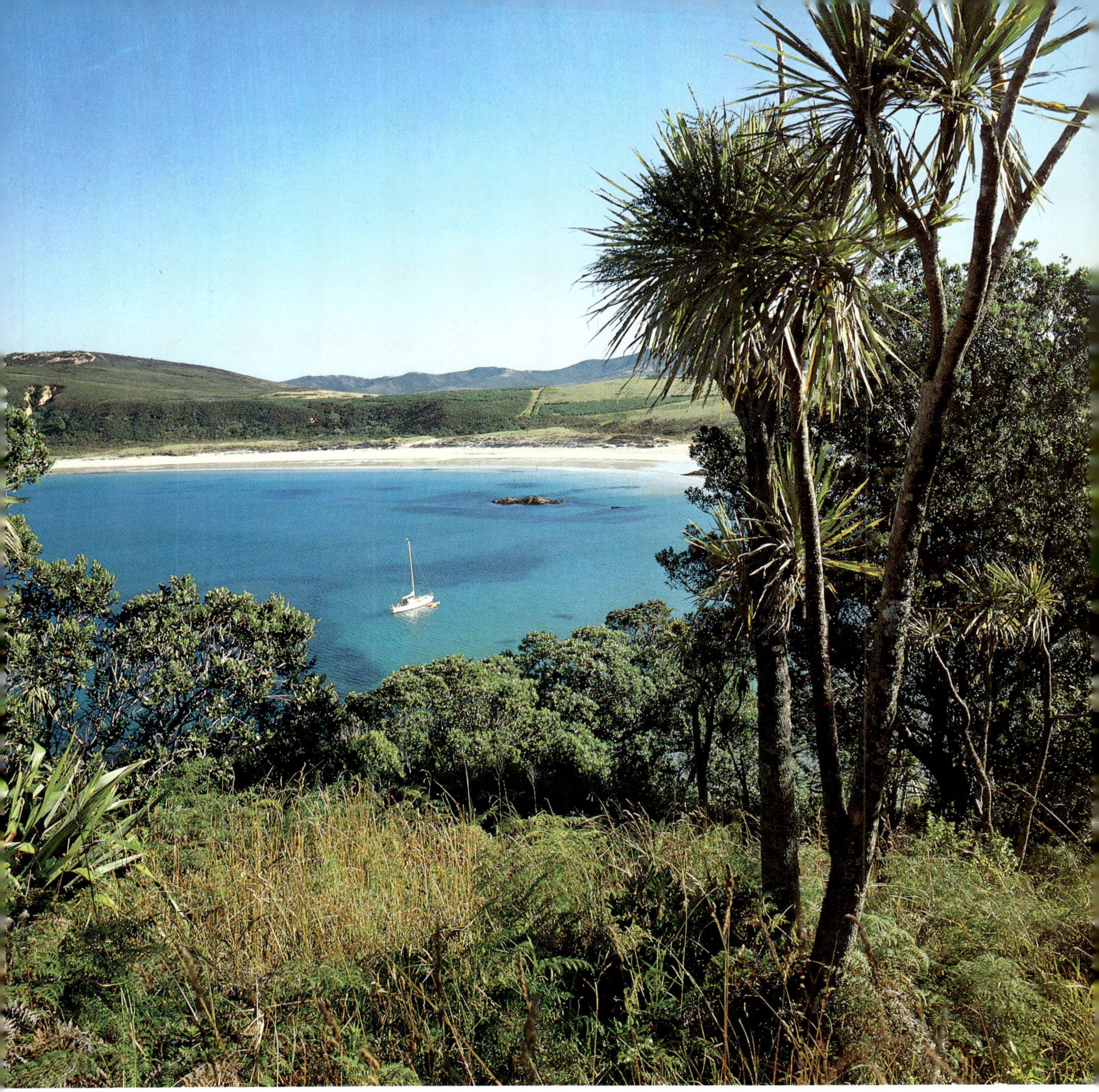

requiring constant dredging, carrying a lively commerce; of mountain wilderness bordered by rolling, green hills and willow-shaded streams in scenes of pastoral peace; of iron-bound coasts interrupted by idyllic bays of near tropical langour, and leaned over by lofty, eternally snow-covered peaks.

Explore it with us through this selection from the endless variety, the vast procession of breathtaking views, of New Zealand in a few of its many, fascinating moods.

Hokianga Harbour, (above, left), slips inland past huge sand dunes and the twin resorts of Omapere and Opononi and winds inland between wooded hills for some 20 miles. Kerikeri, (left), site of earliest missionary activity, is a river basin anchorage for small craft on the Bay of Islands coast. Matai Bay, near Cape Kari Kari, (above), though deep and sheltered, sees few vessels other than pleasure craft.

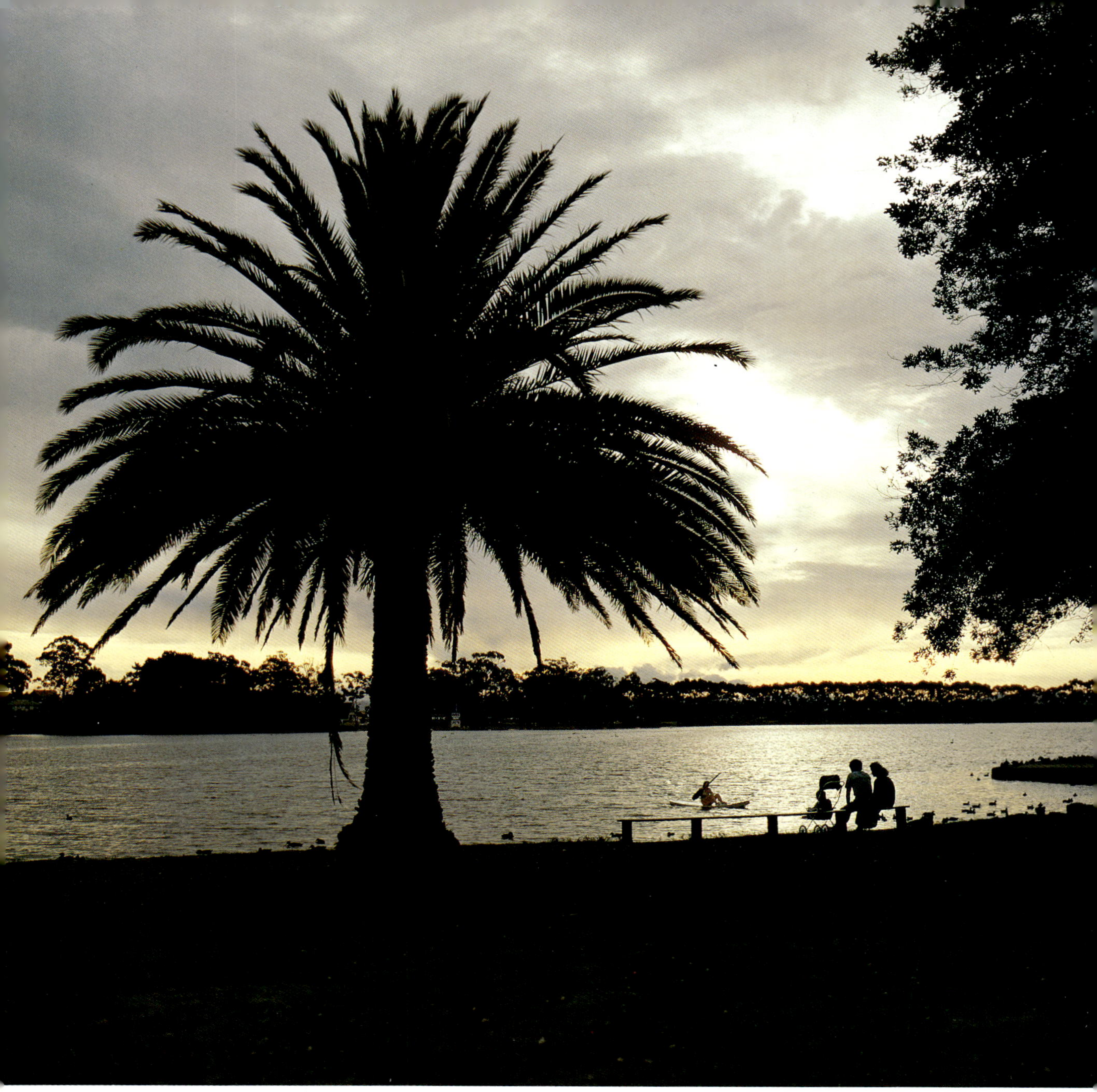

Hamilton is a small-town-become-city which has retained gracious residential areas and beautiful parks, like Rotorua, (above), with its lovely lake, complete with picnic and bathing facilities. Averaging 30km in width, its highest point just over 840m, its hills once rich in gold and now richly fertile pasture, and its steep-sided, twisty valleys often filled with luxuriant forest including even the mighty **kauri,** the Coromandel Peninsula is highly favoured by generous Nature. The sheer beauty of its forests and hills and seascapes, the peace of its glorious beaches and sheltered coves, and its kindly climate make it ideal for holidaying, and an idyllic place in which to live.

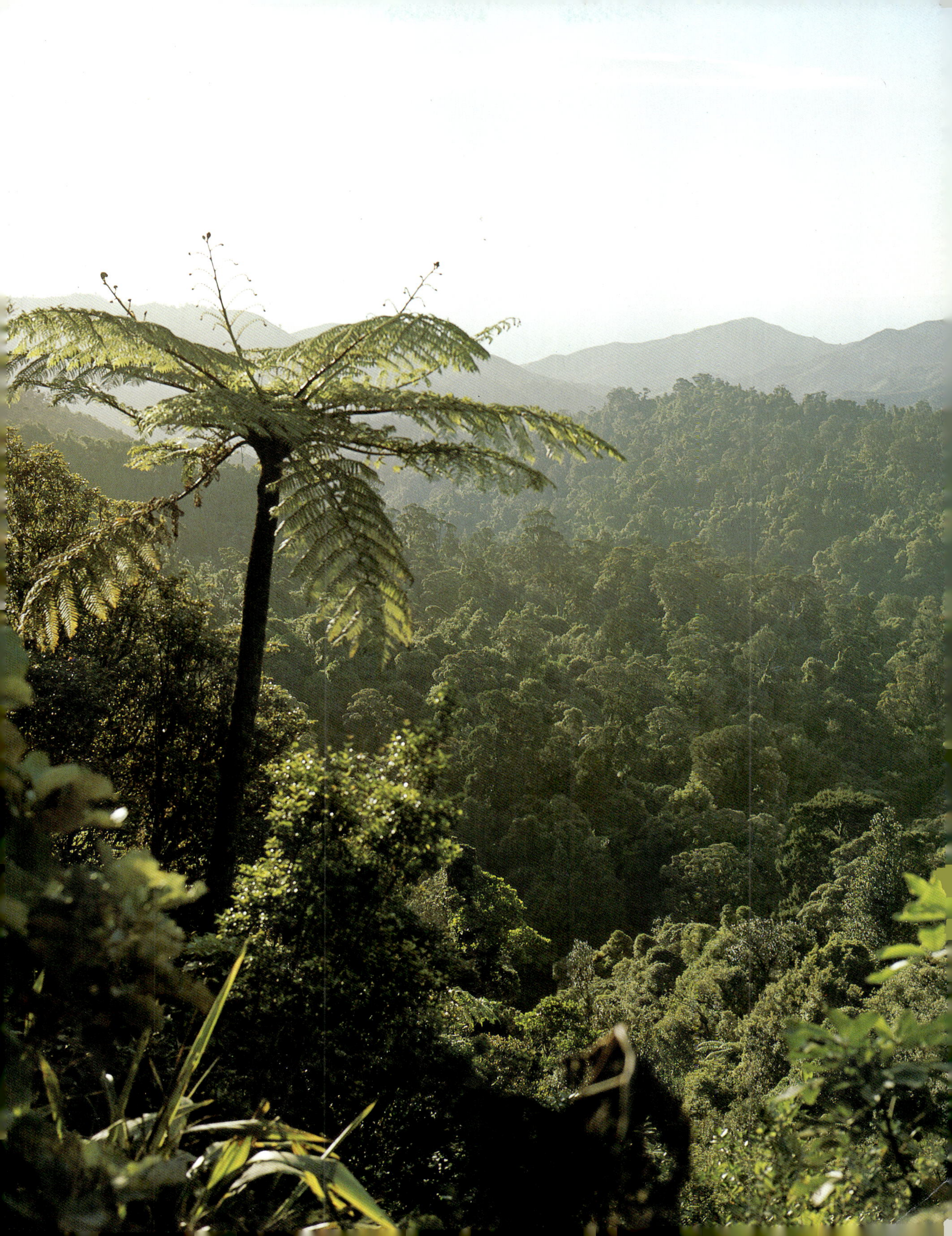

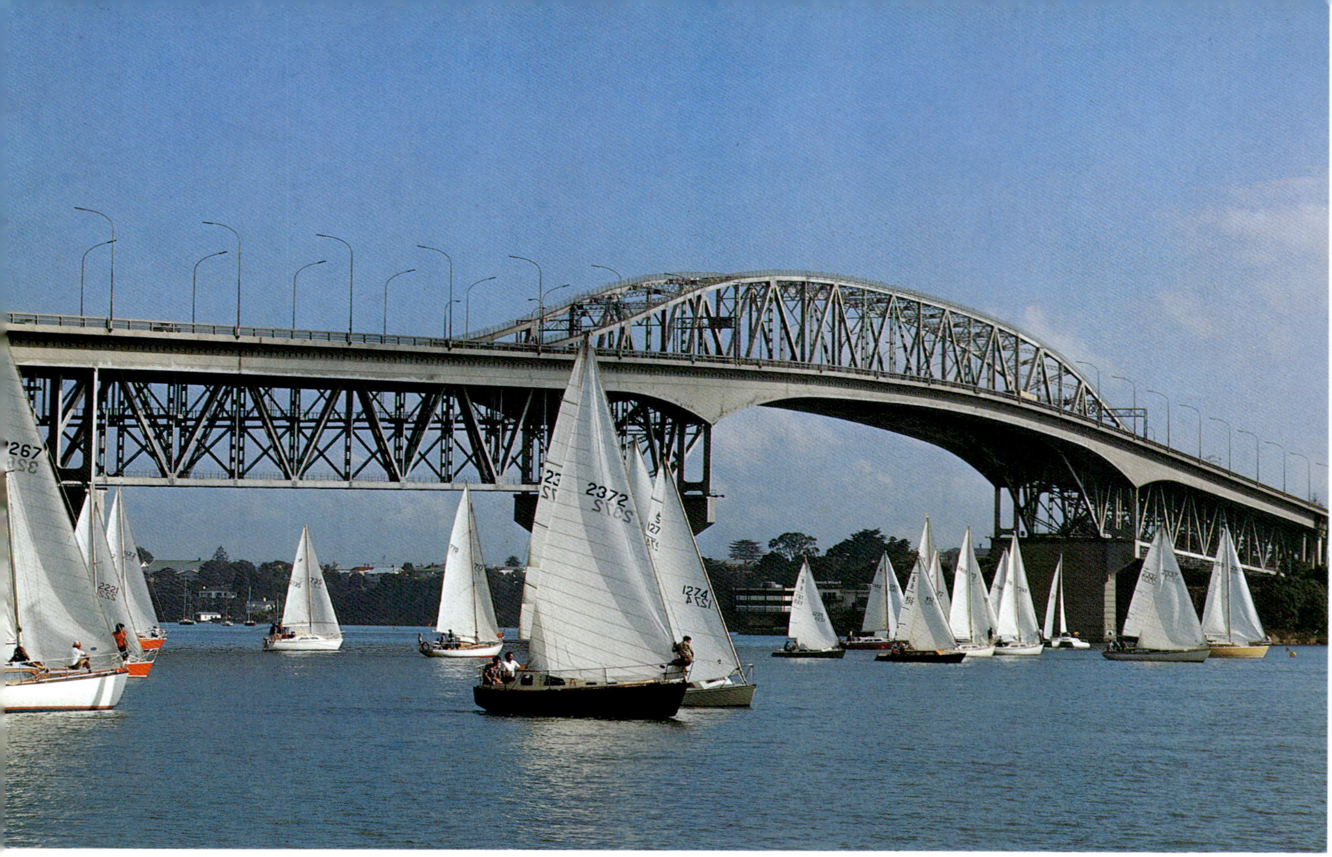
2372
1274

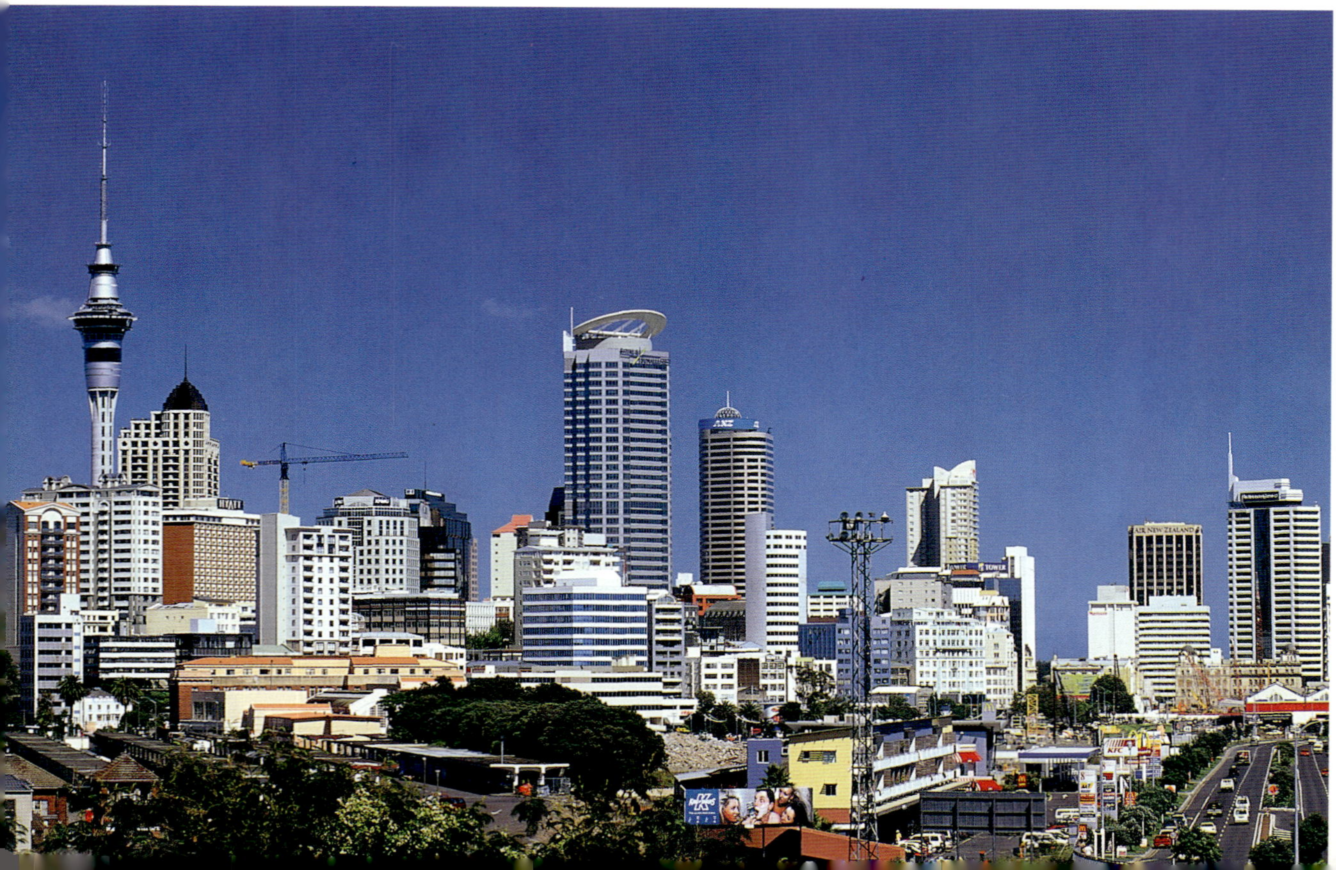

Auckland, superbly sited on the Waitemata Harbour, provides its million citizens with all the facilities for a delightfully outdoor lifestyle (yachting, upper left), the sophisticated amenities of a big city (lower left), and a scalloped coastline offering get-away-from-it-all peace, as here at Mahurangi Bay, just an hour's journey from the city centre.

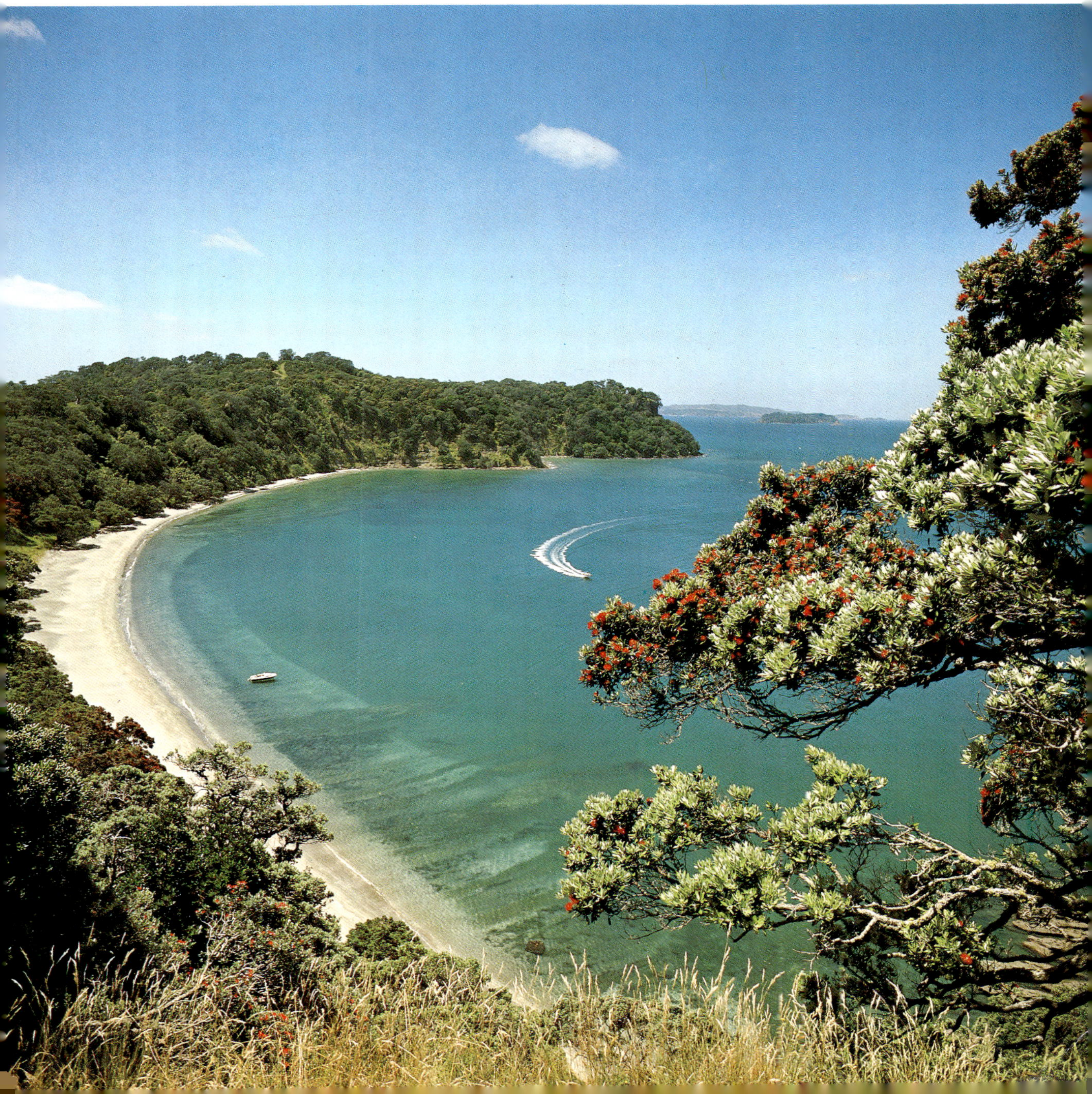

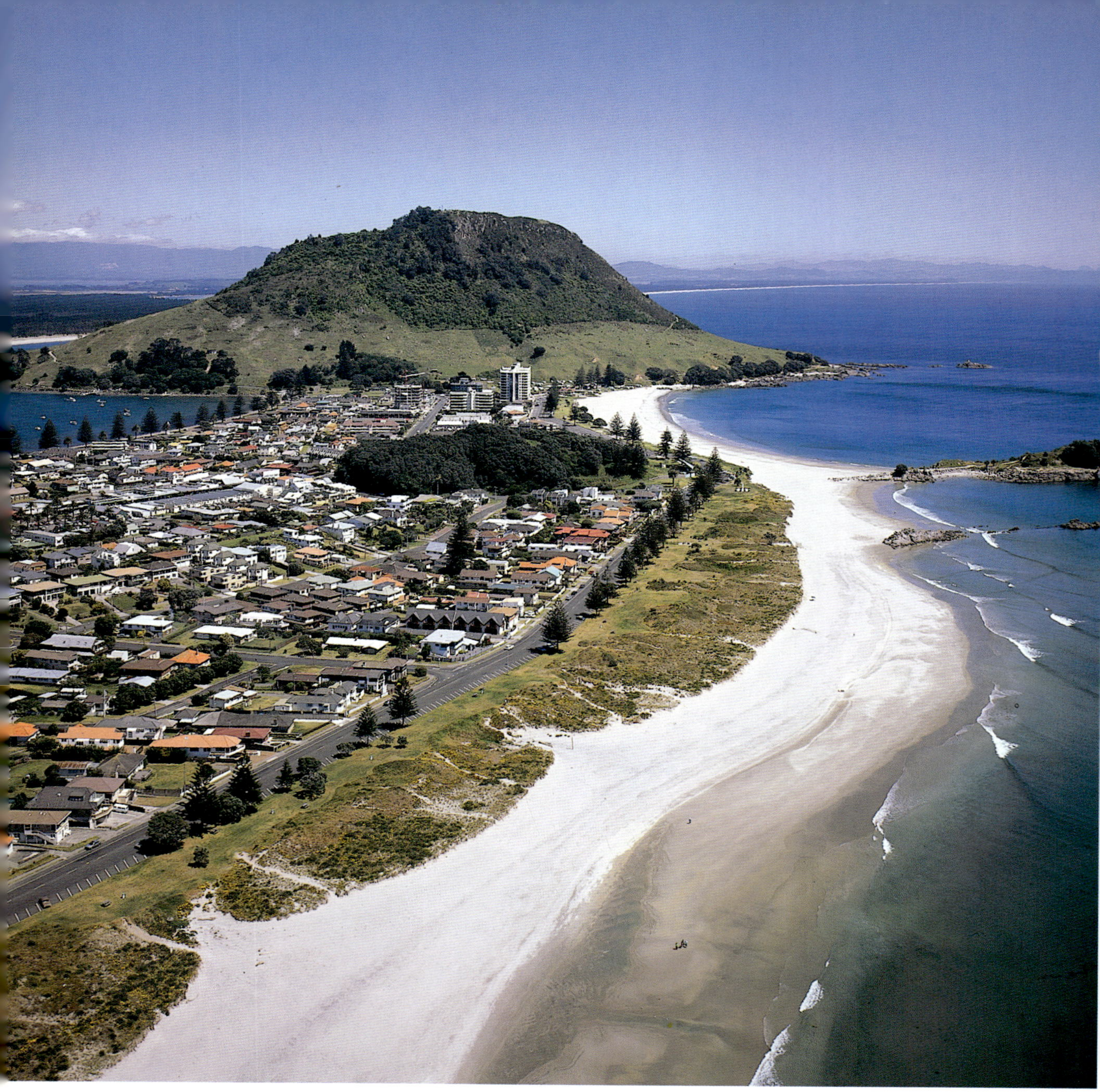

A magnificent surfing beach along a narrow neck of land connects Mount Maunganui's 232m bulk with the mainland, and forms a natural breakwater between the open sea and Tauranga Harbour; and Cook's Bay and Lonely Beach, (right), a sheltered pair of beautiful coves, provided a calm anchorage for Captain Cook when he established an observatory here to observe the transit of Mercury in 1769.

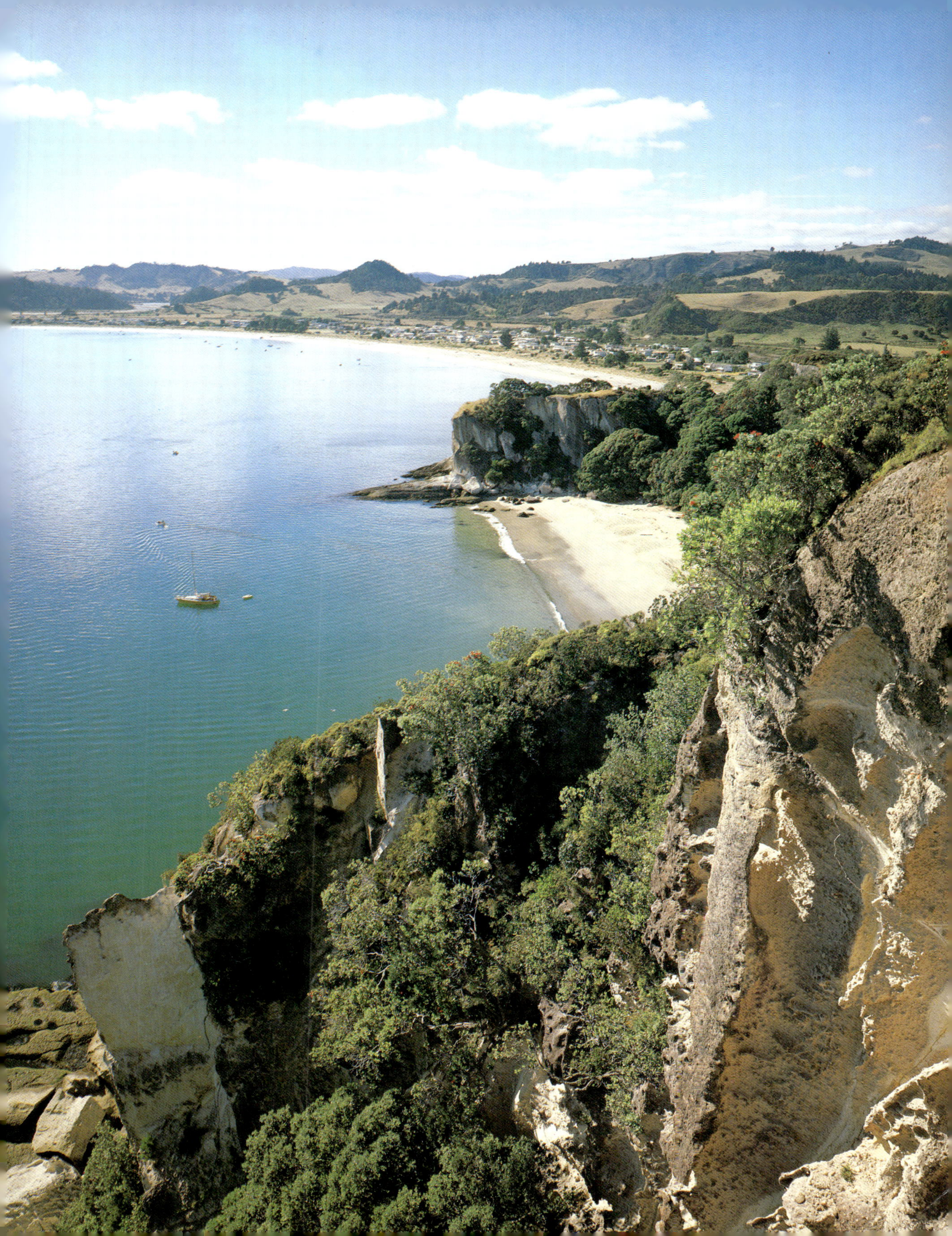

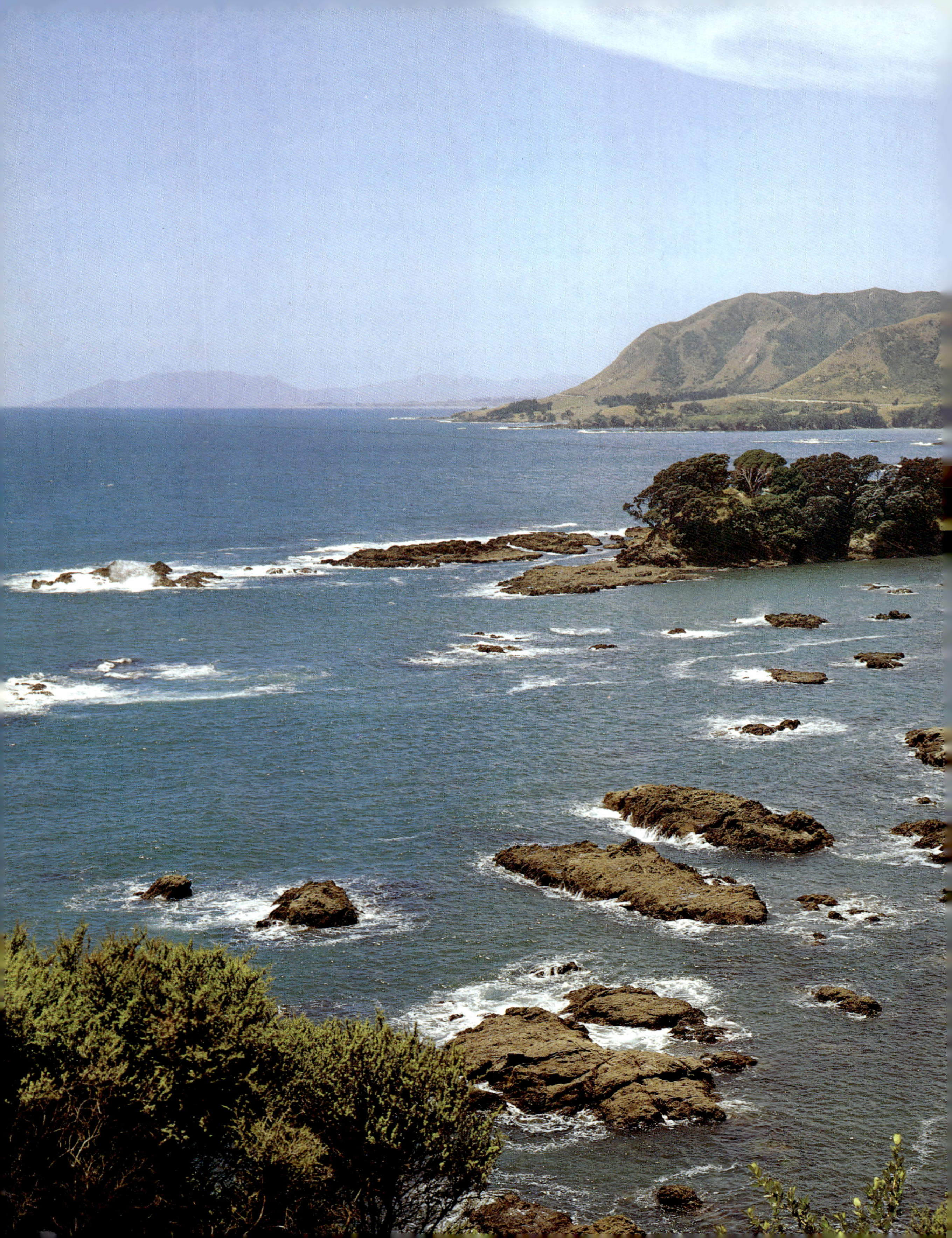

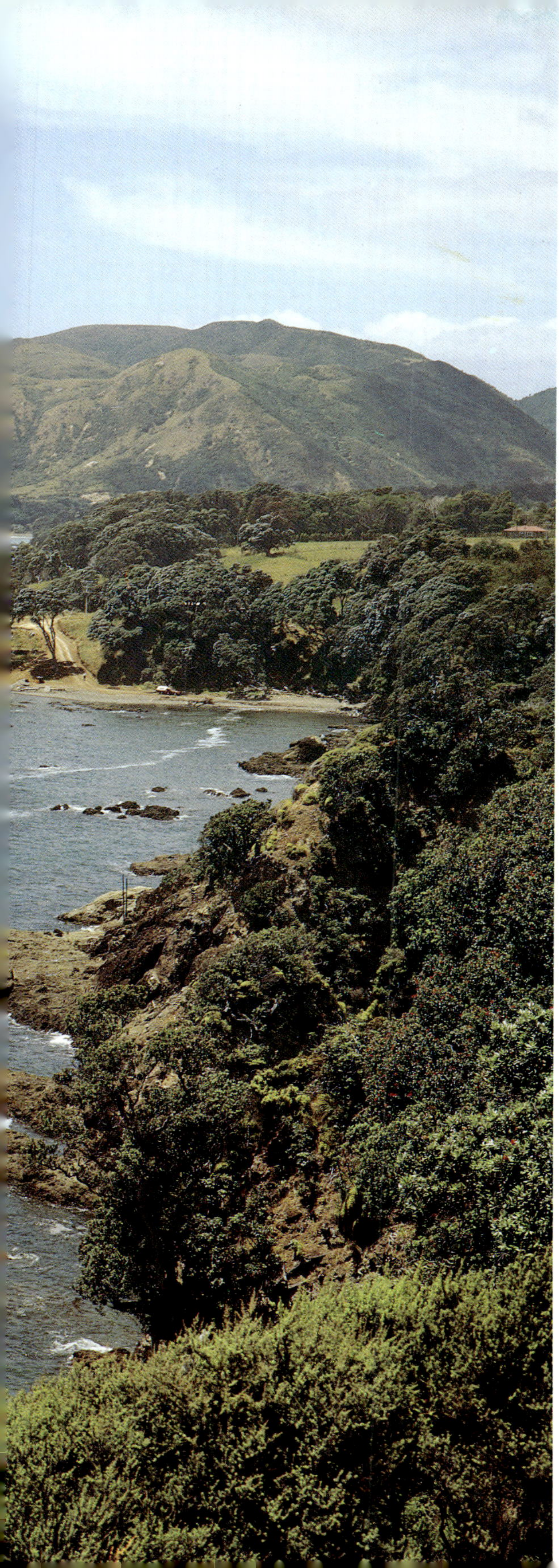

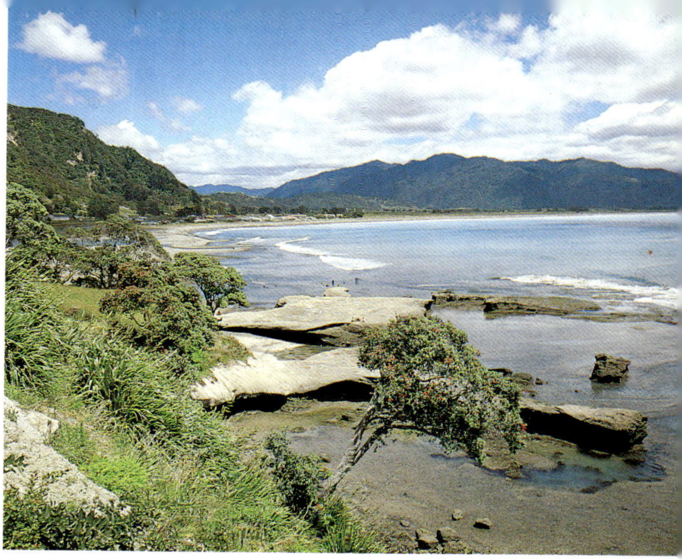

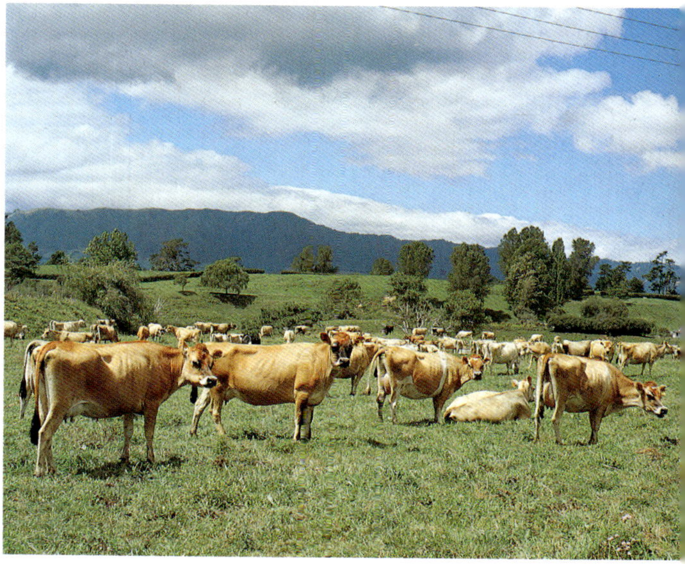

Te Araroa township crouches beneath a lofty scarp where the Awatere River rushes out from the highlands and spills into Kawakawa Bay, top right, famous for the size and age of its pohutukawa trees. Whanarua Bay, (left), seventy miles away by road, on the Bay of Plenty coast, is a series of reef-bound inlets, renowned for fishing; and the westerly winds and the high Kaimai ranges which overlook the Bay of Plenty coast combine to produce a rainfall which makes the Waikato a rich dairying country, (lower right.)

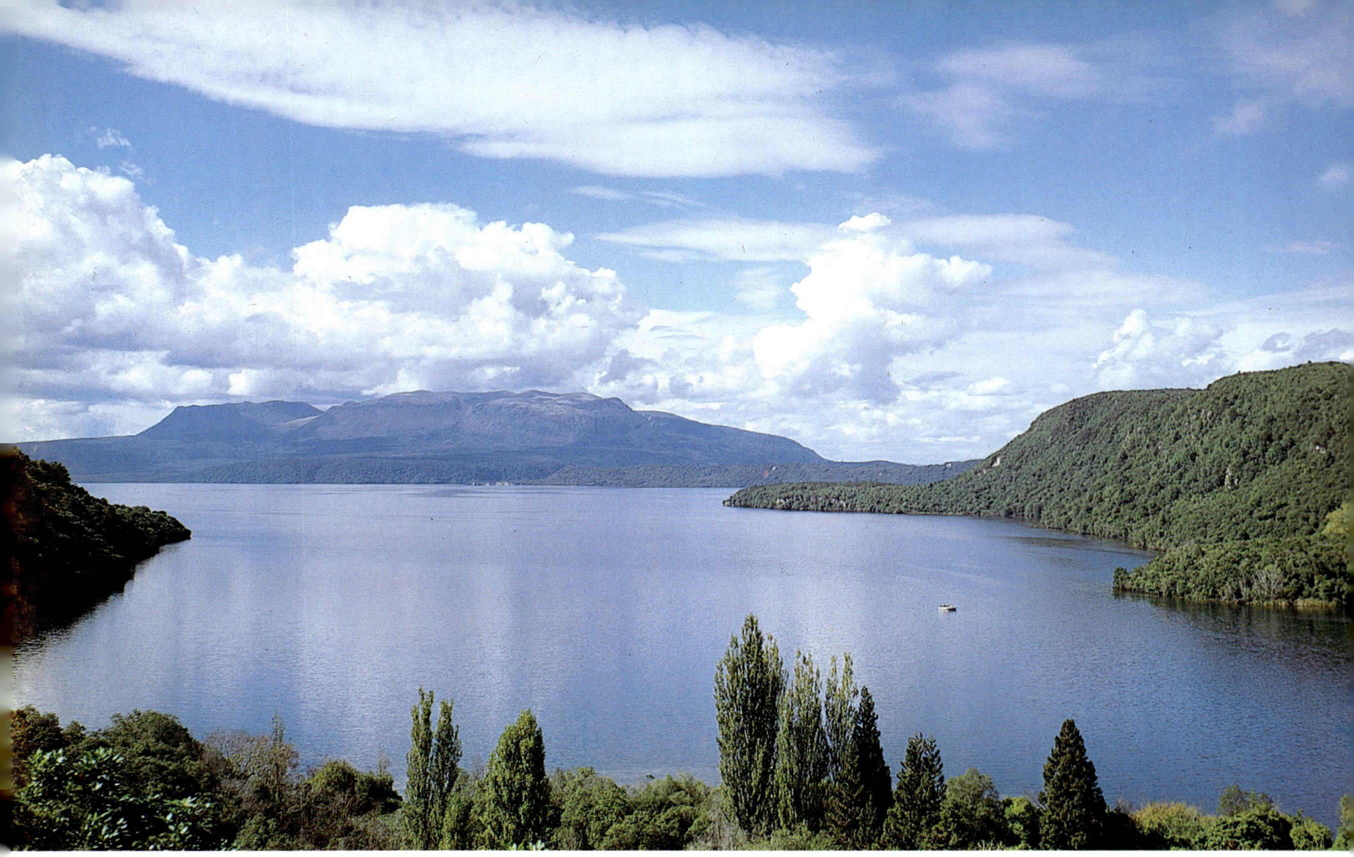

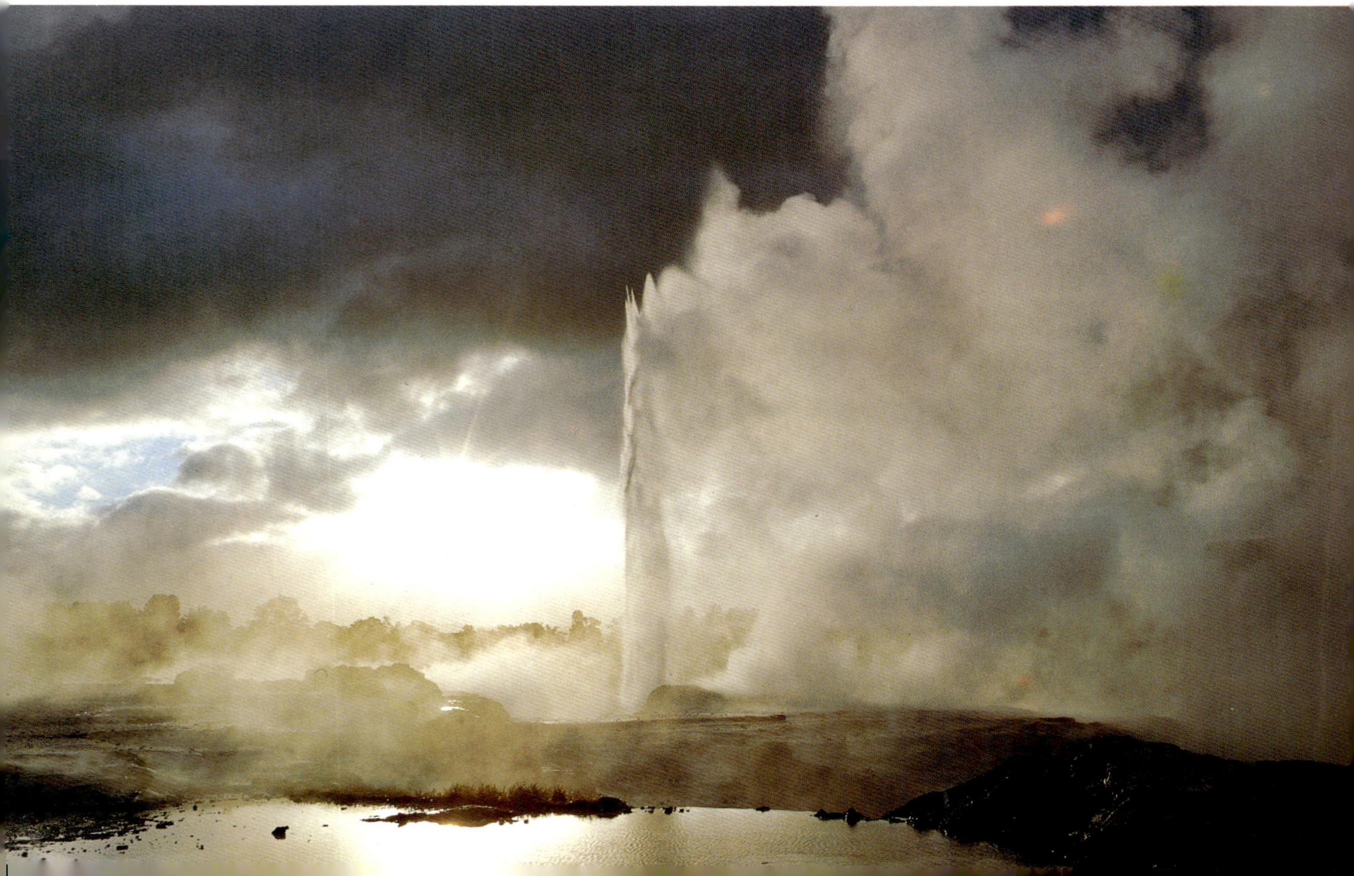

Lake Tarawera, (top left), 15 square miles of peaceful water, spreads beneath the shattered bulk of Mt. Tarawera, which erupted in 1886, burying the village of Te Wairoa on a terrace above this lovely shore. Geysers at Whakarewarewa, (lower left), testify to the fact that such titanic forces still exist; and the Craters of the Moon at Wairakei (below), suggest something of their awesome power.

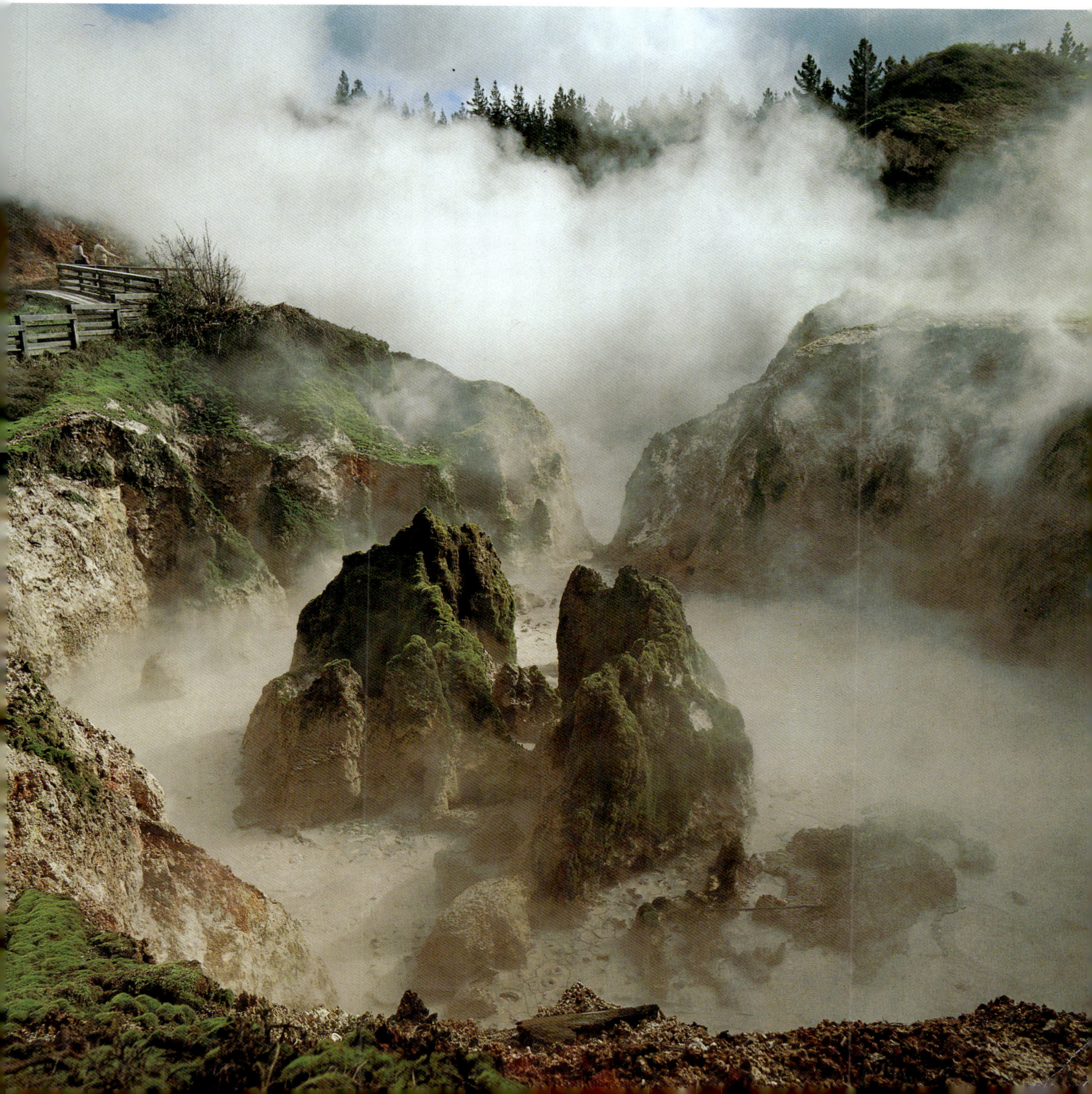

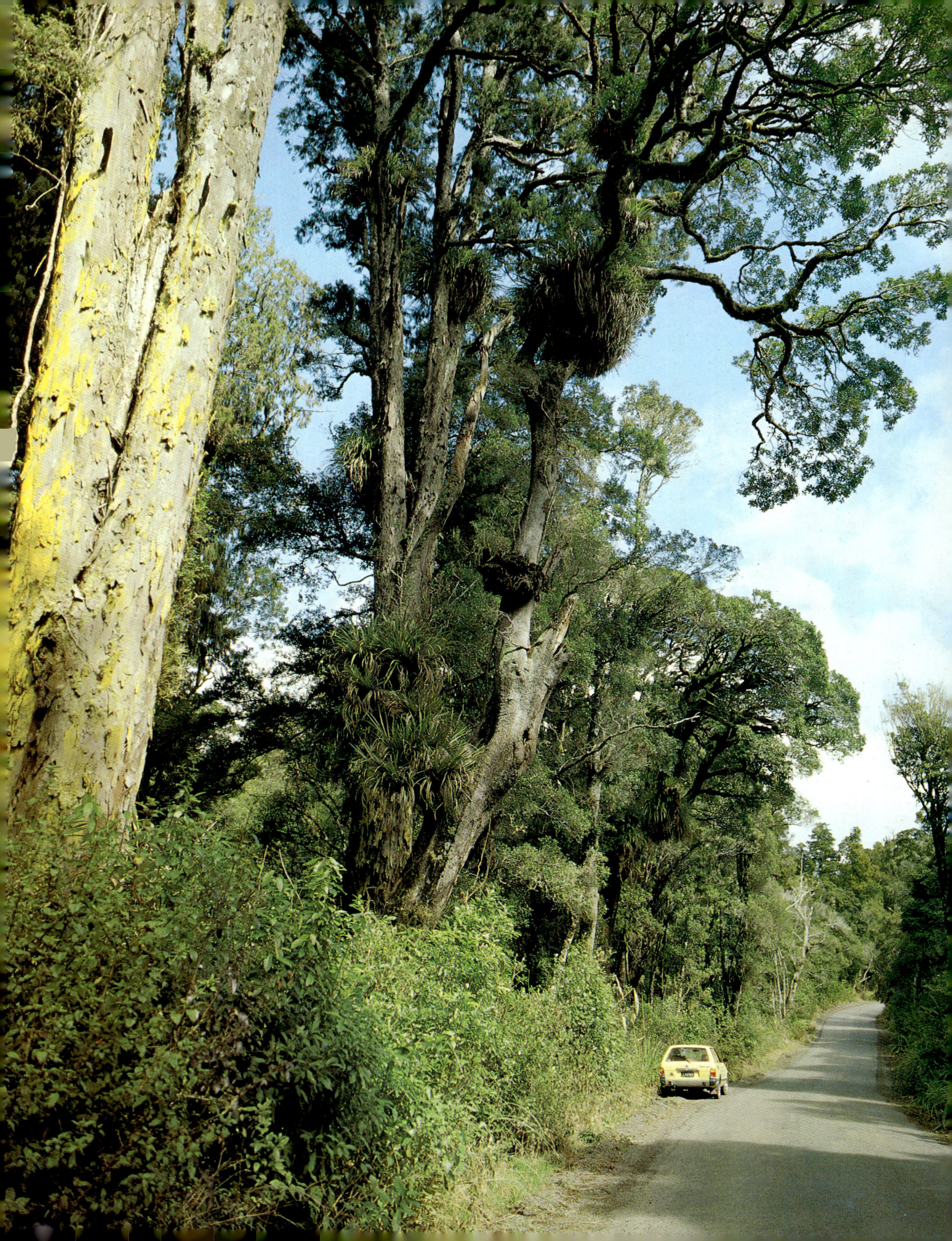

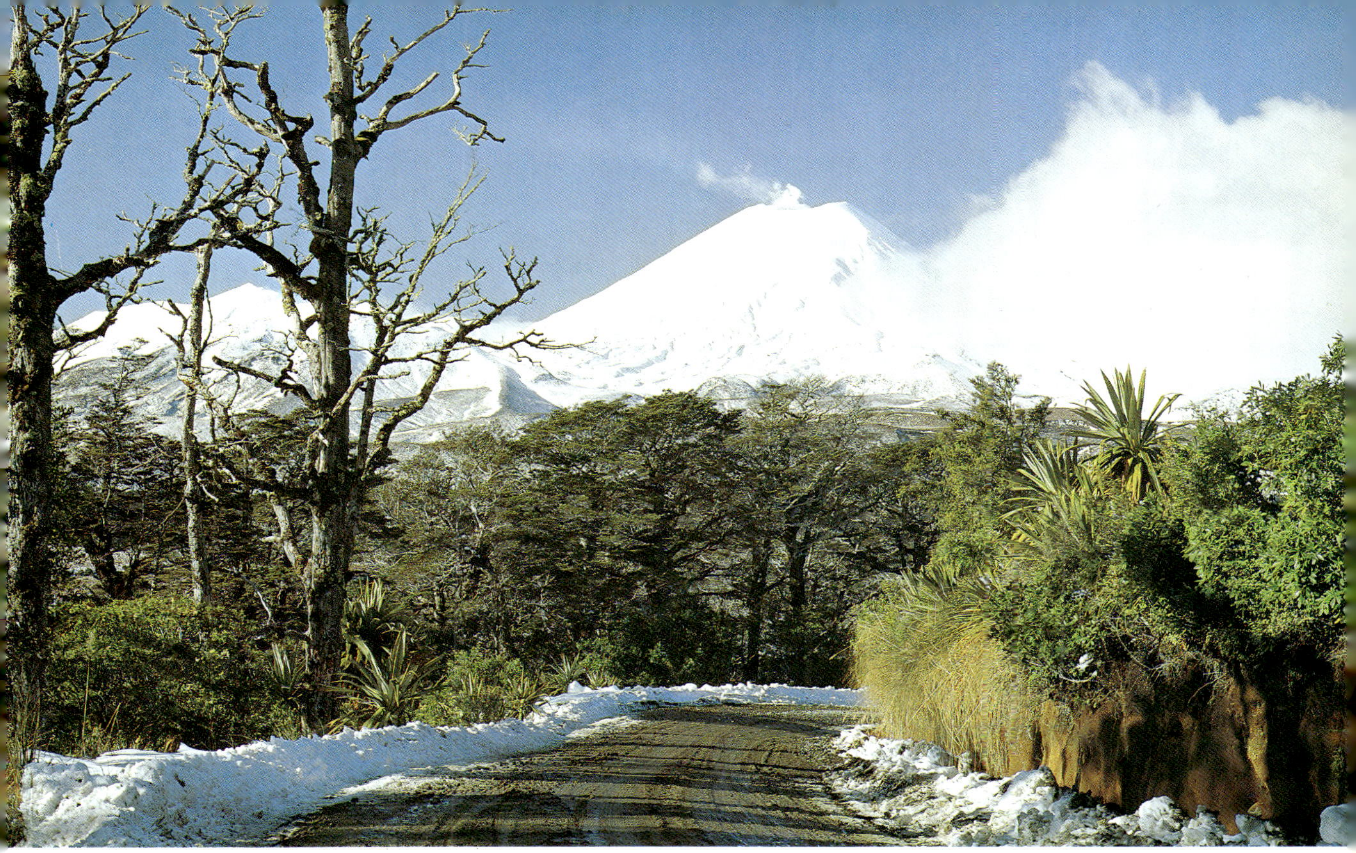

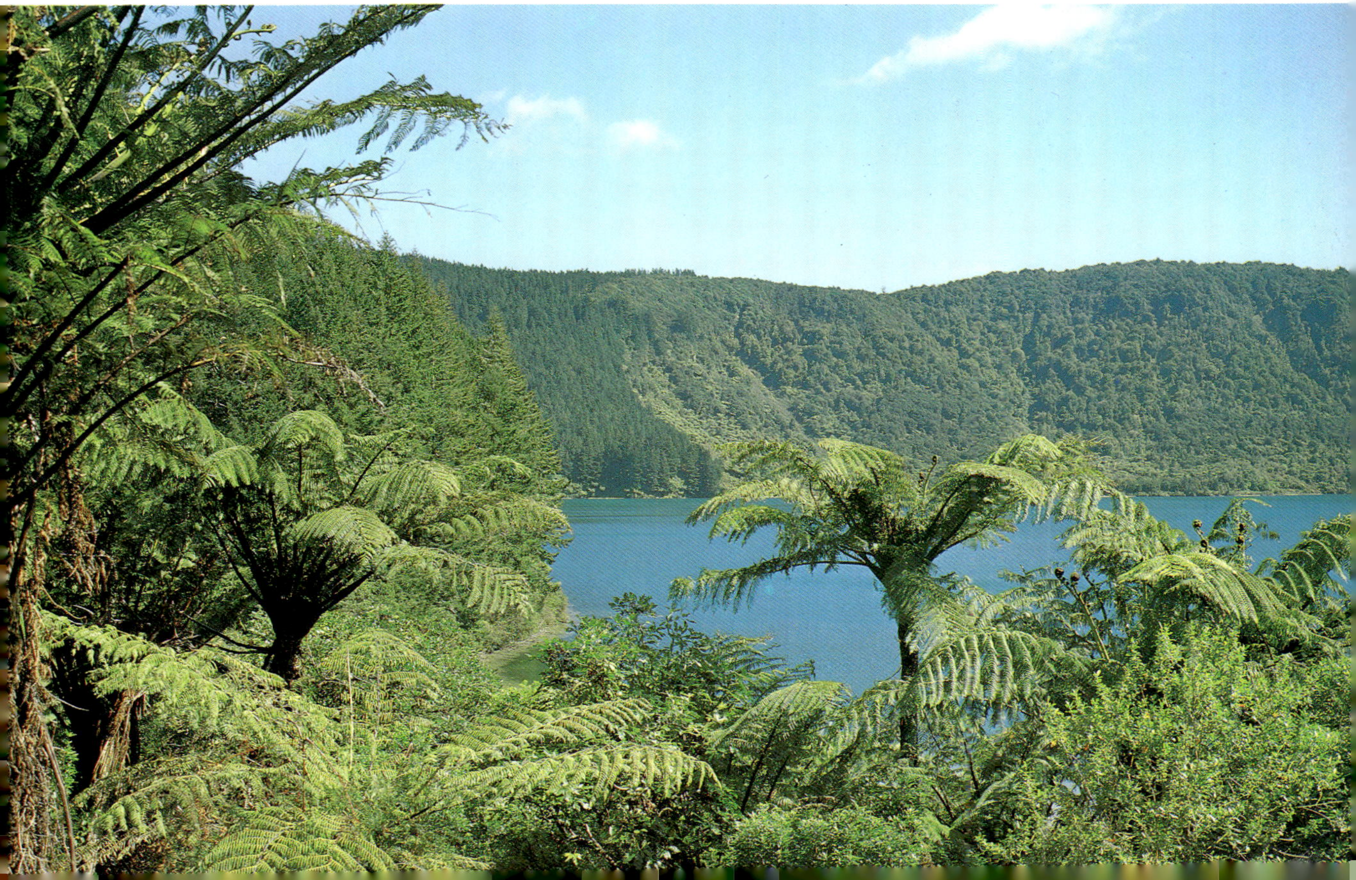

Previous page.
It is one of the glories of New Zealand mountain scenery that the way to the skifields can run through luxuriant forest, as here at the Turoa Skifields, (above); that the frozen slopes of the mountains climb right to the lips of volcanic craters, as on Mt. Ngauruhoe, (upper right); and that the lesser hills of the volcanic heart of the North Island hide their scars under luxuriant forest, and cradle in their valleys lakes like Tikitapu, clear and intensely blue from the mineral content of the water, (lower right.)

The Huka Falls, (below), are not noted for their height, nor even for their size, but rather for their savage power as the Waikato River rushes down a rock-bedded incline some 229m long, with a drop over that distance of 8m, to plunge over an 11m ledge. Mount Egmont, (right), a dormant volcano, is spoken of as New Zealand's Fujiyama; but it has a less symetrical cone than Fuji. The rugged, bush-clad hills to the right are the shattered remains of a similar cone.

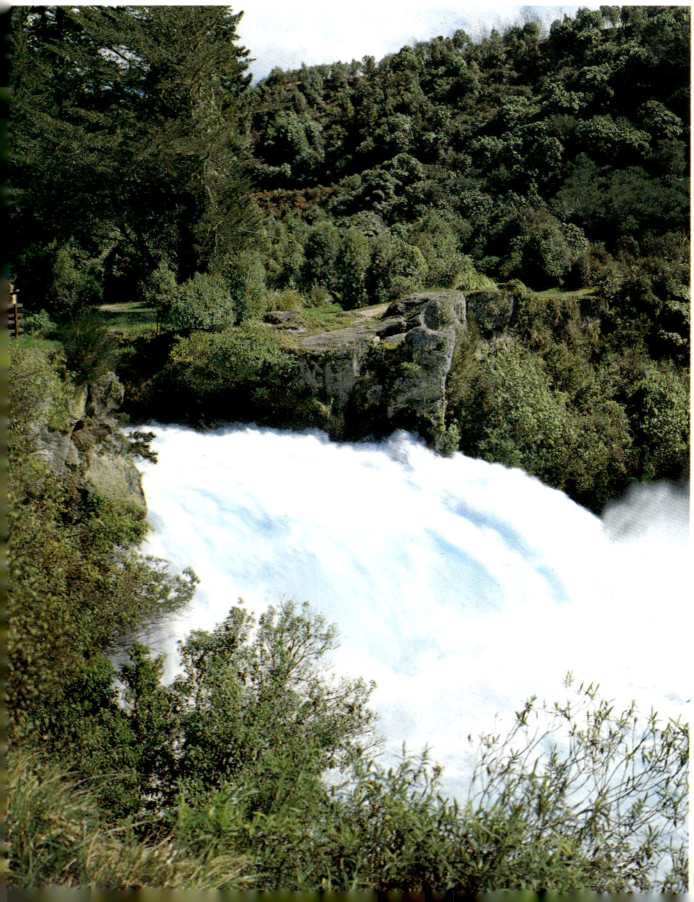

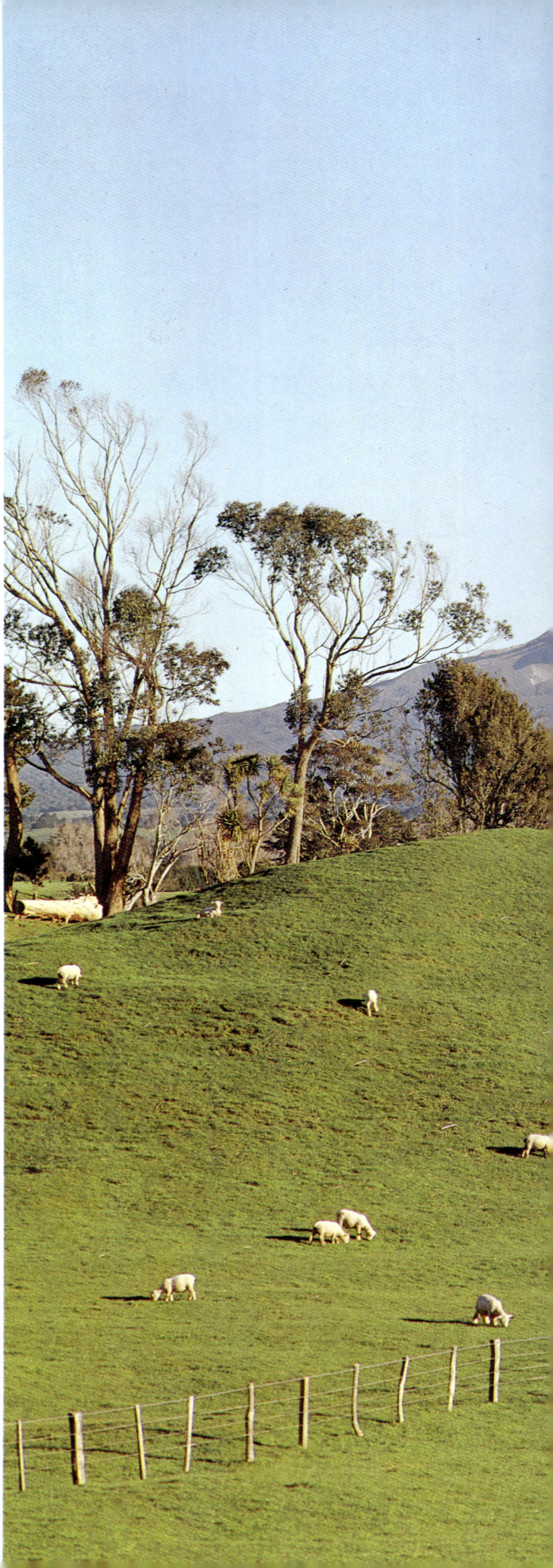

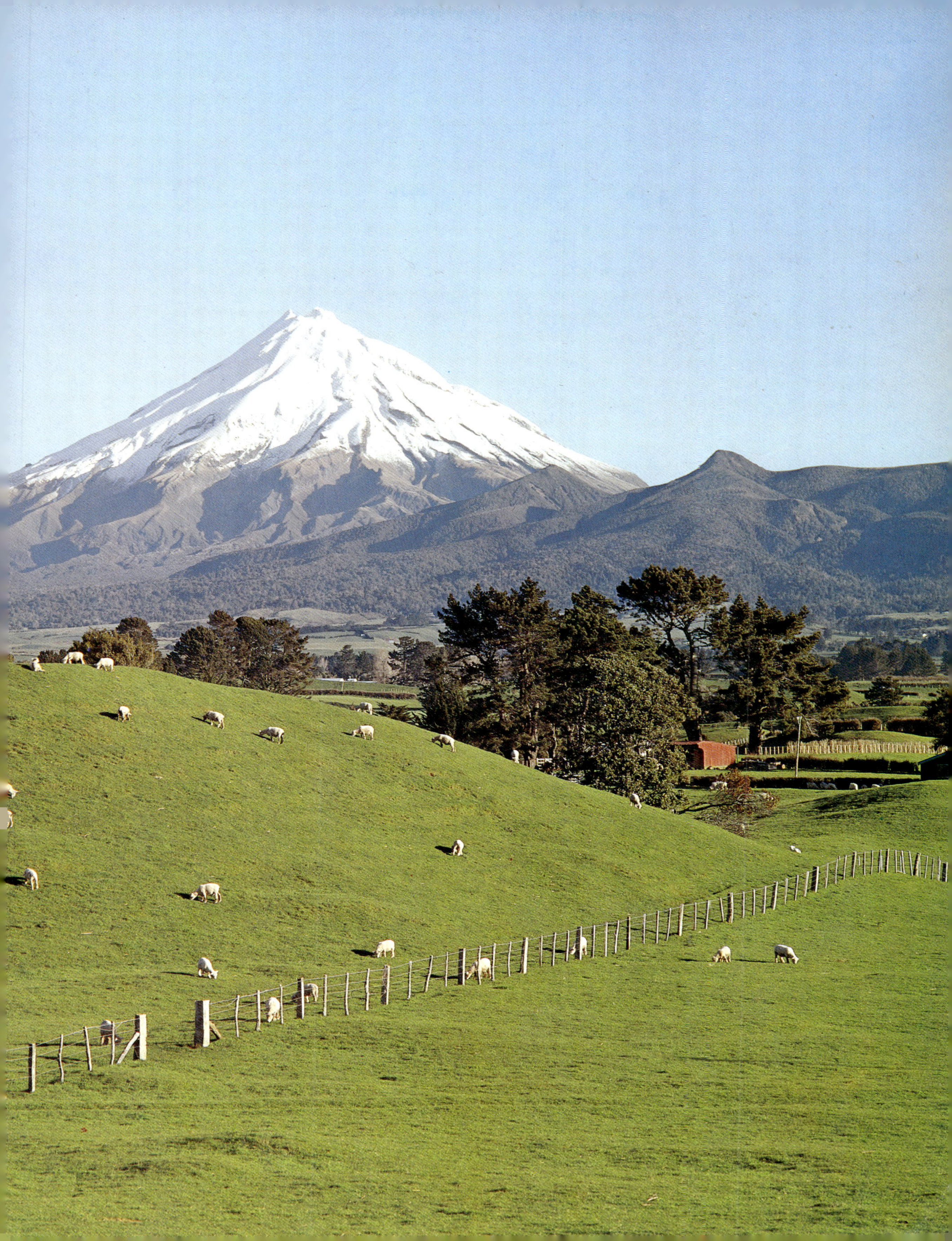

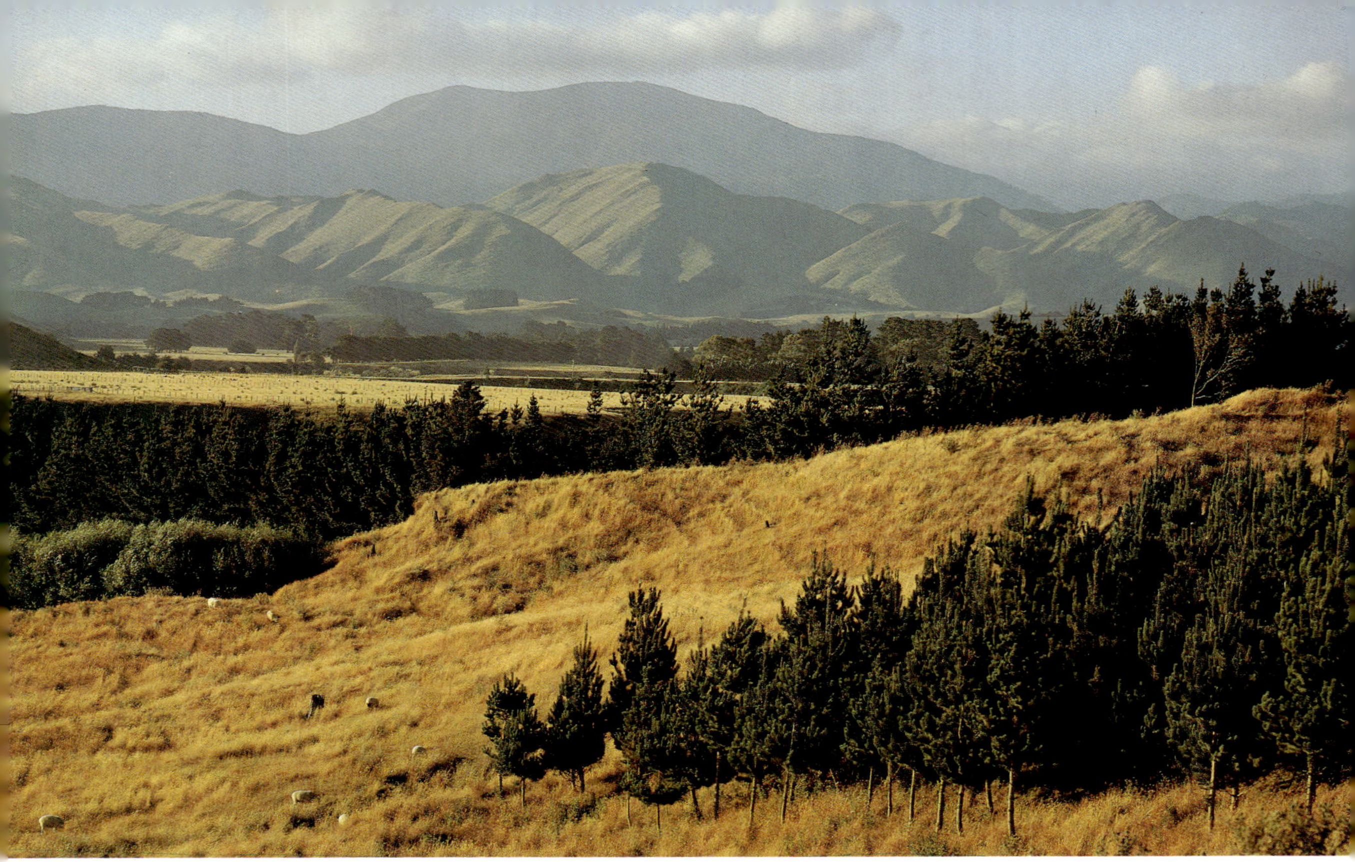

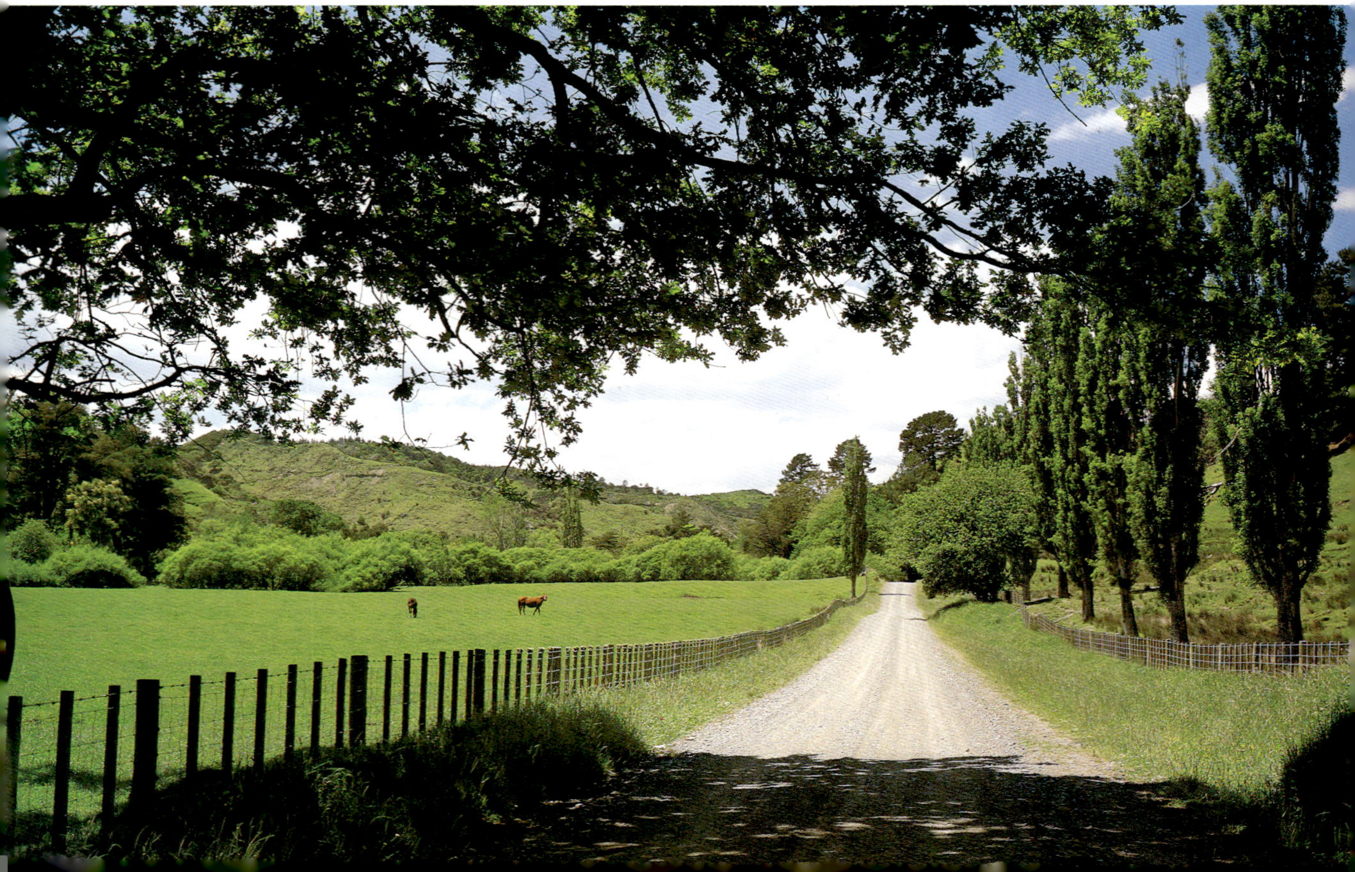

The Ruahine Range, (top left), stops abruptly at the Manawatu Gorge, western gateway to Hawkes Bay, where the Manawatu River steadily wears its way through, separating the still-rising Ruahine and Tararua Ranges. On the west coast, the gentle Kaukatea Valley, (lower left), borders the broken, forested country east and north of Wanganui; and on the east coast, the coastal hills run down to the sea at Cape Kidnappers, (below), in a series of swooping ridges, where gannets maintain two of their rare mainland nesting colonies.

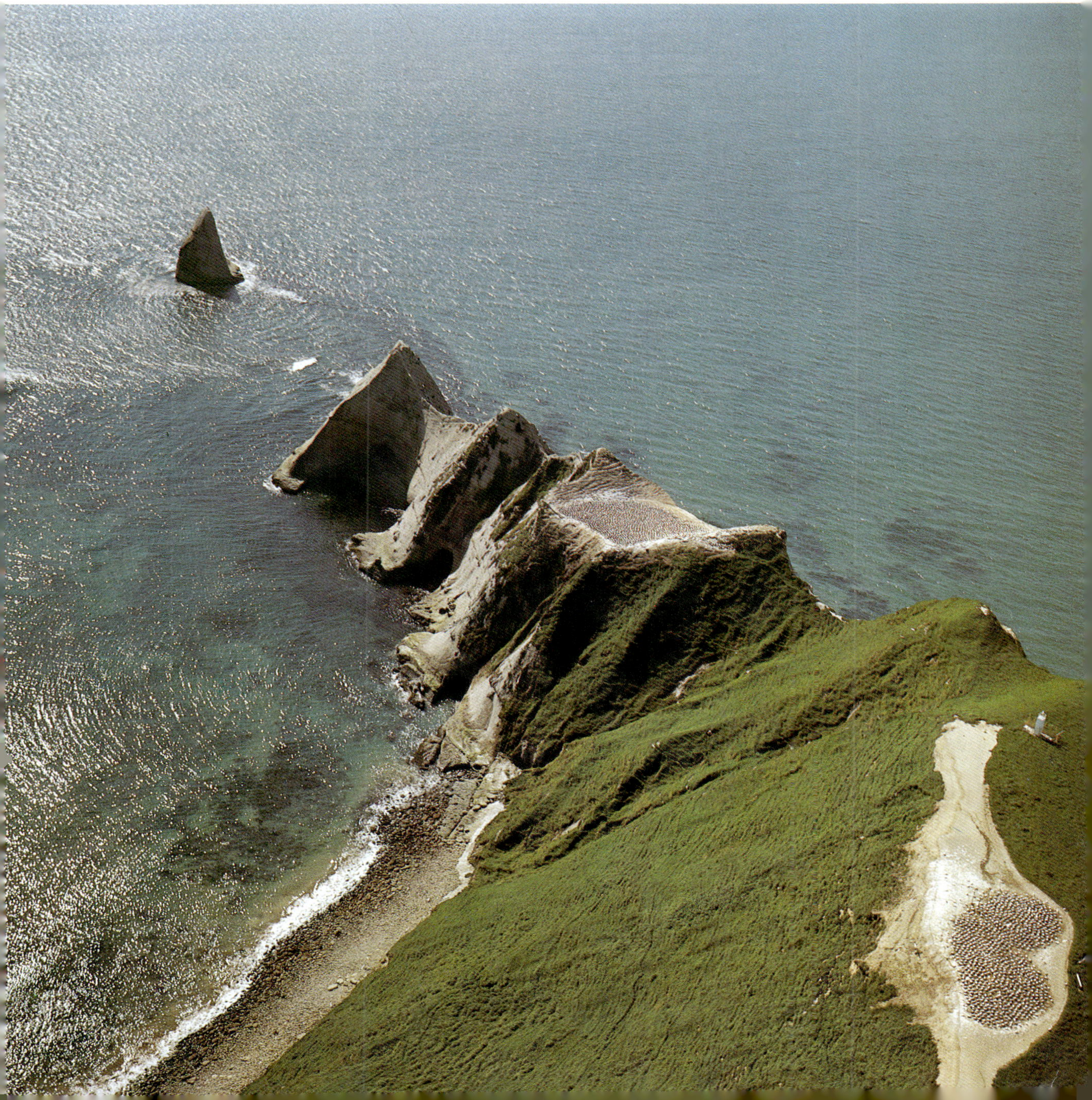

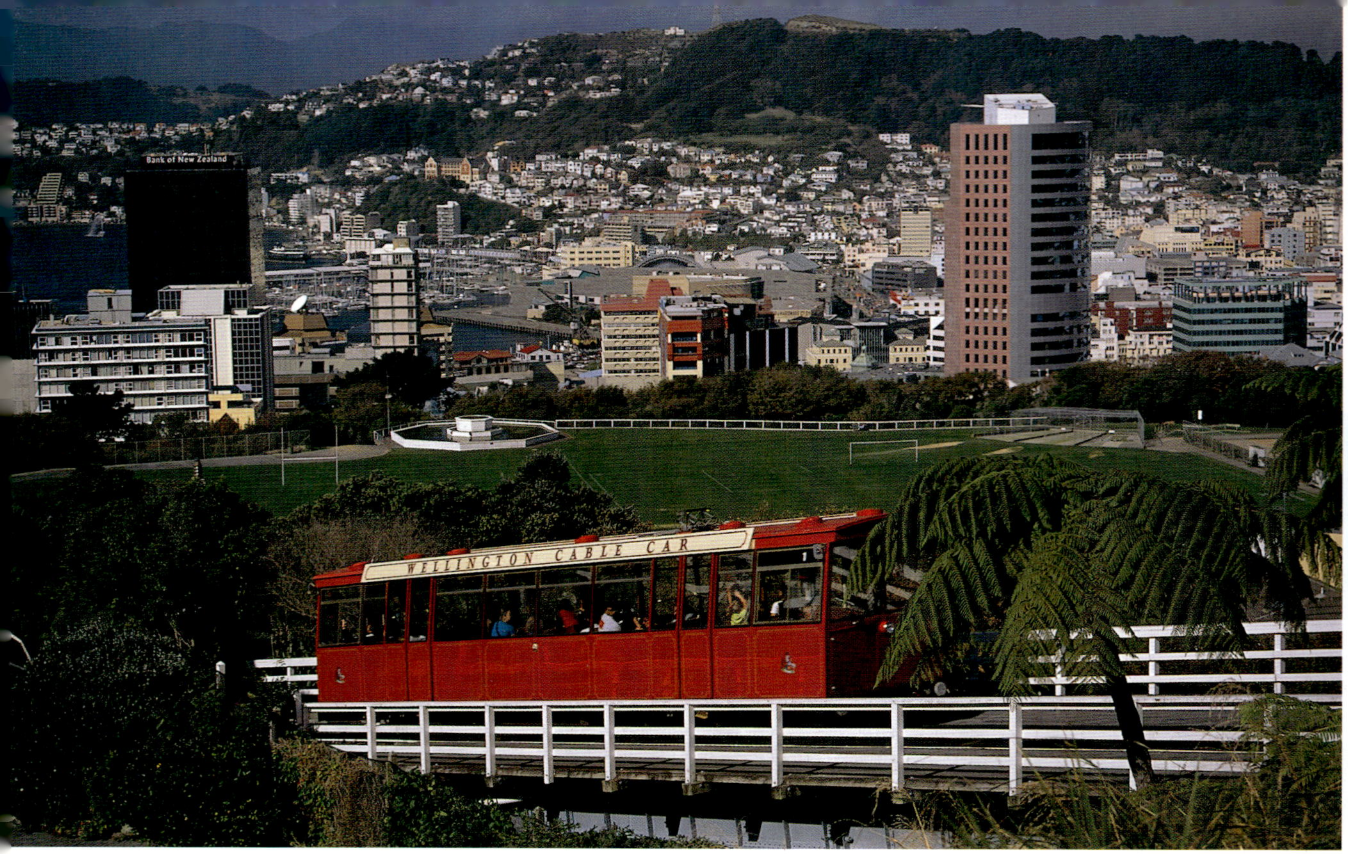
Bank of New Zealand
WELLINGTON CABLE CAR

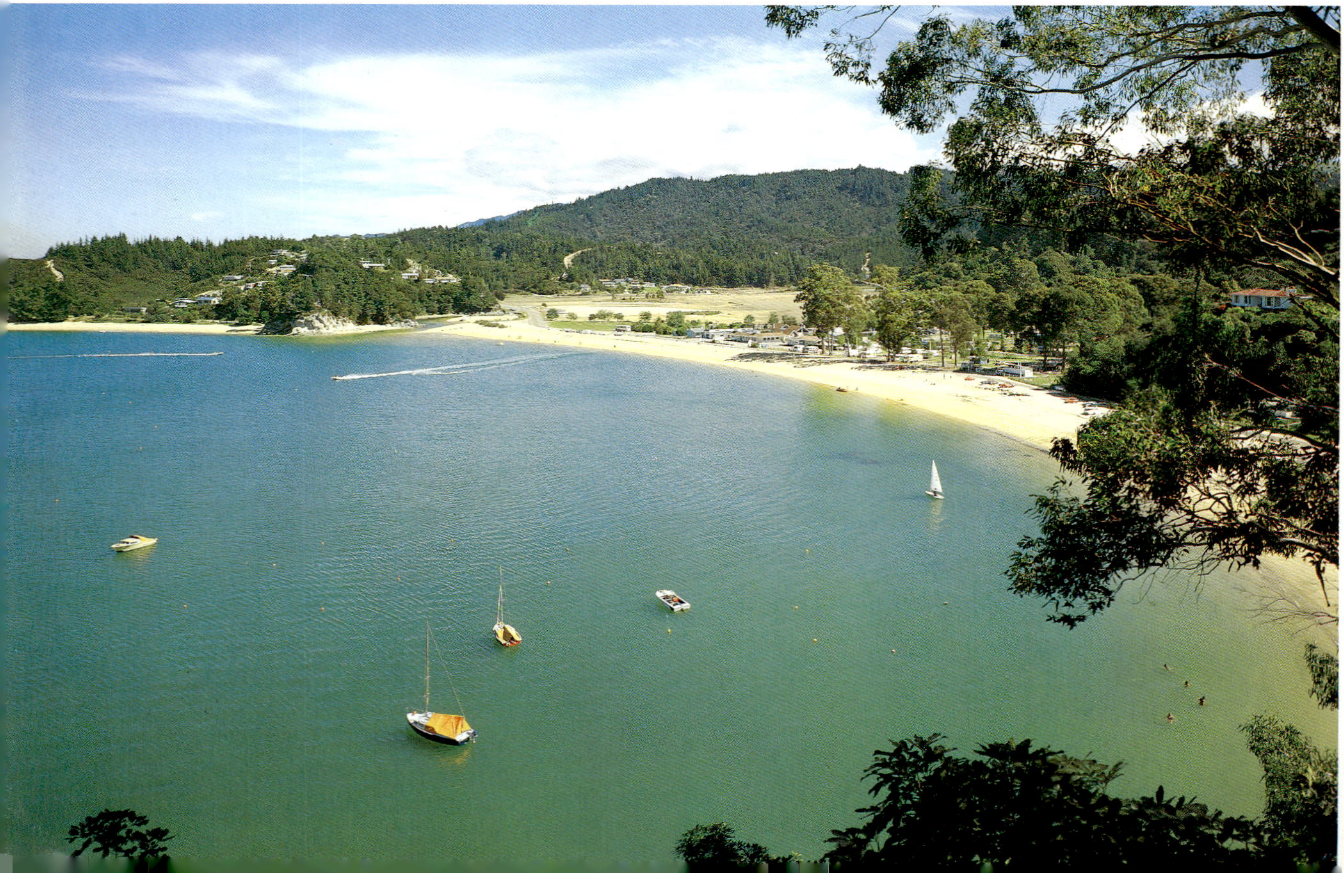

Wellington, (top left), on the southern tip of the North Island, curls about its beautiful harbour, crowding its business and administrative centre onto a narrow strip of reclaimed land close to the waterfront. Kaiteriteri, (bottom left), in the north of the South Island, spreads itself about a beautiful, gently-shelving bay; and in the drowned valleys of the Marlborough Sounds, Mt. Shewell rears its forested top above the deep waterways of Pelorus, one of the two main inlets. (below)

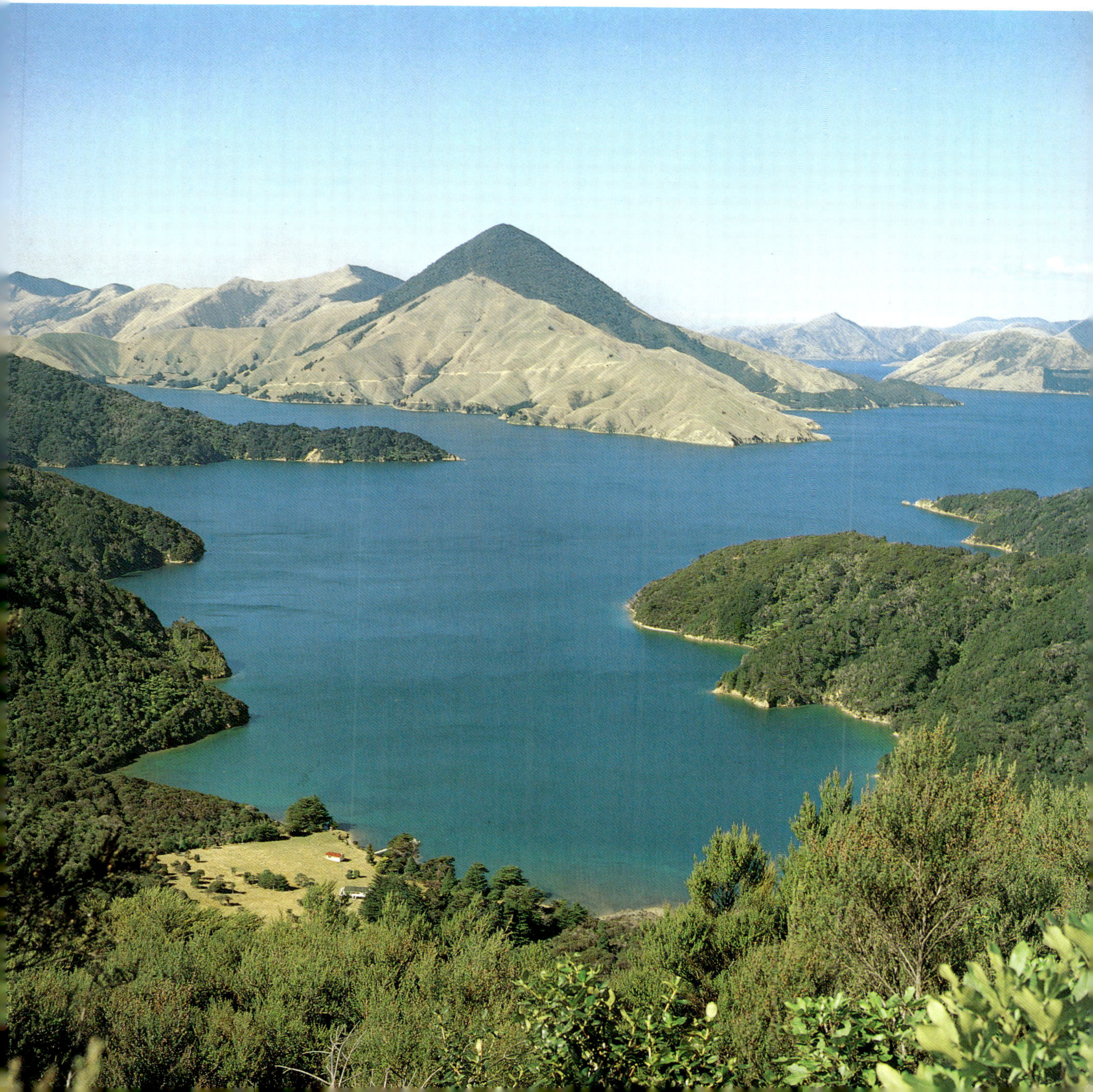

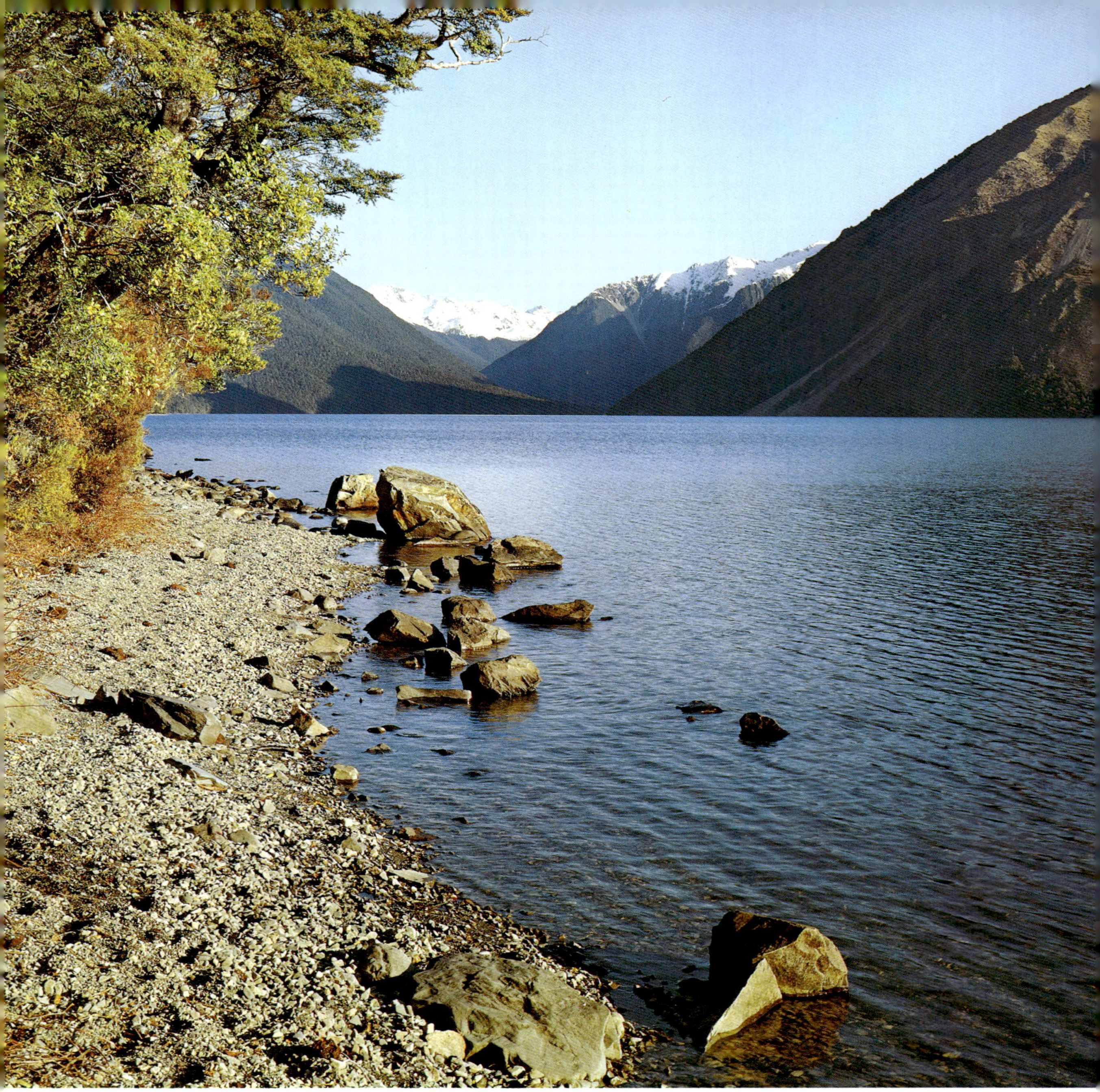

The titanic forces which shaped New Zealand are evident in Lake Rotoiti, (above), occupying a glacial valley beneath the lofty St. Arnaud Range; the mountain valleys drowned by massive subsidence and the rising of the sea level as the last Ice Age passed, to form Queen Charlotte Sound, (above, right), here viewed from Picton's foreshore; and the bizarre Pancake Rocks at Punakaiki, (lower right), on the west coast, carved by wave action of the stormy Tasman Sea.

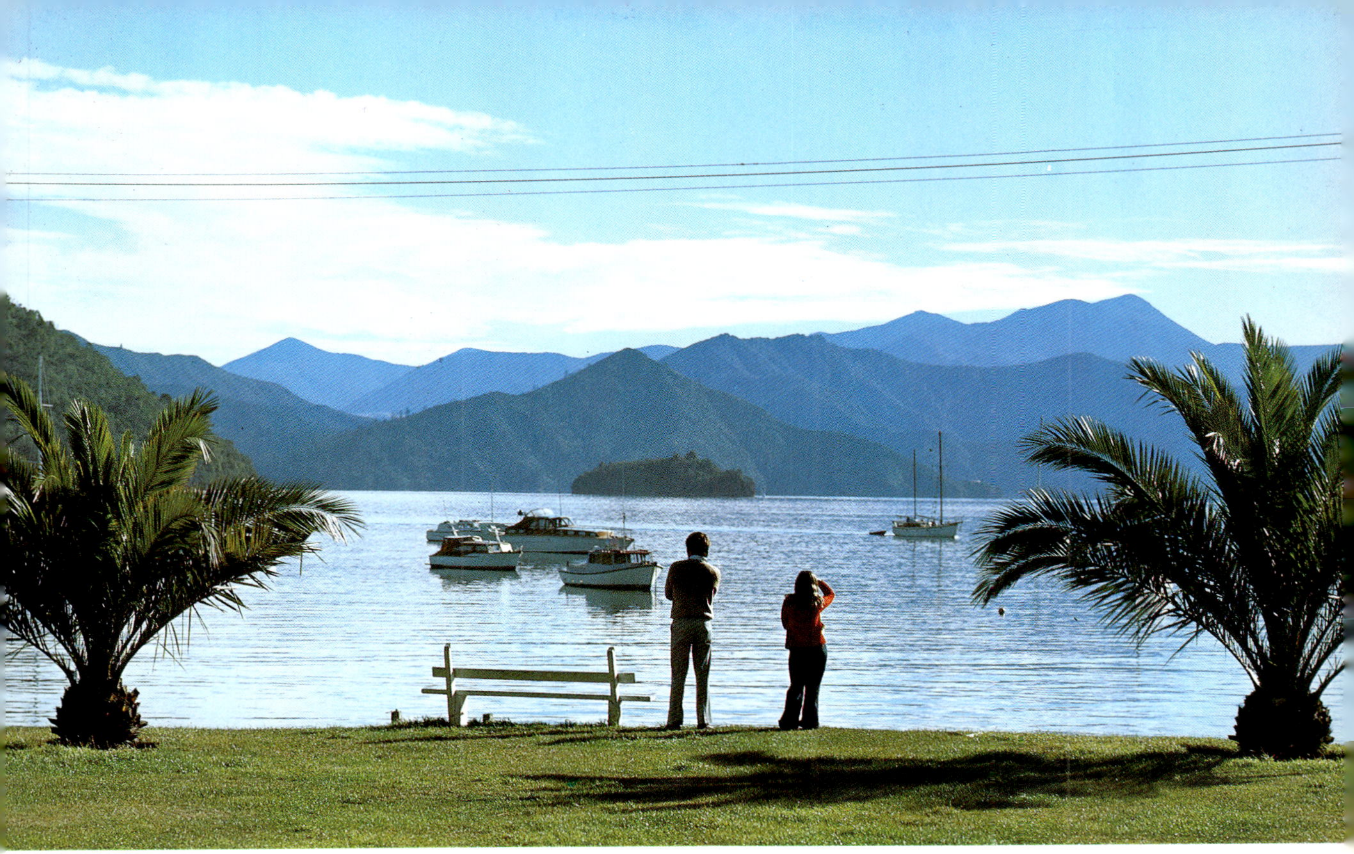
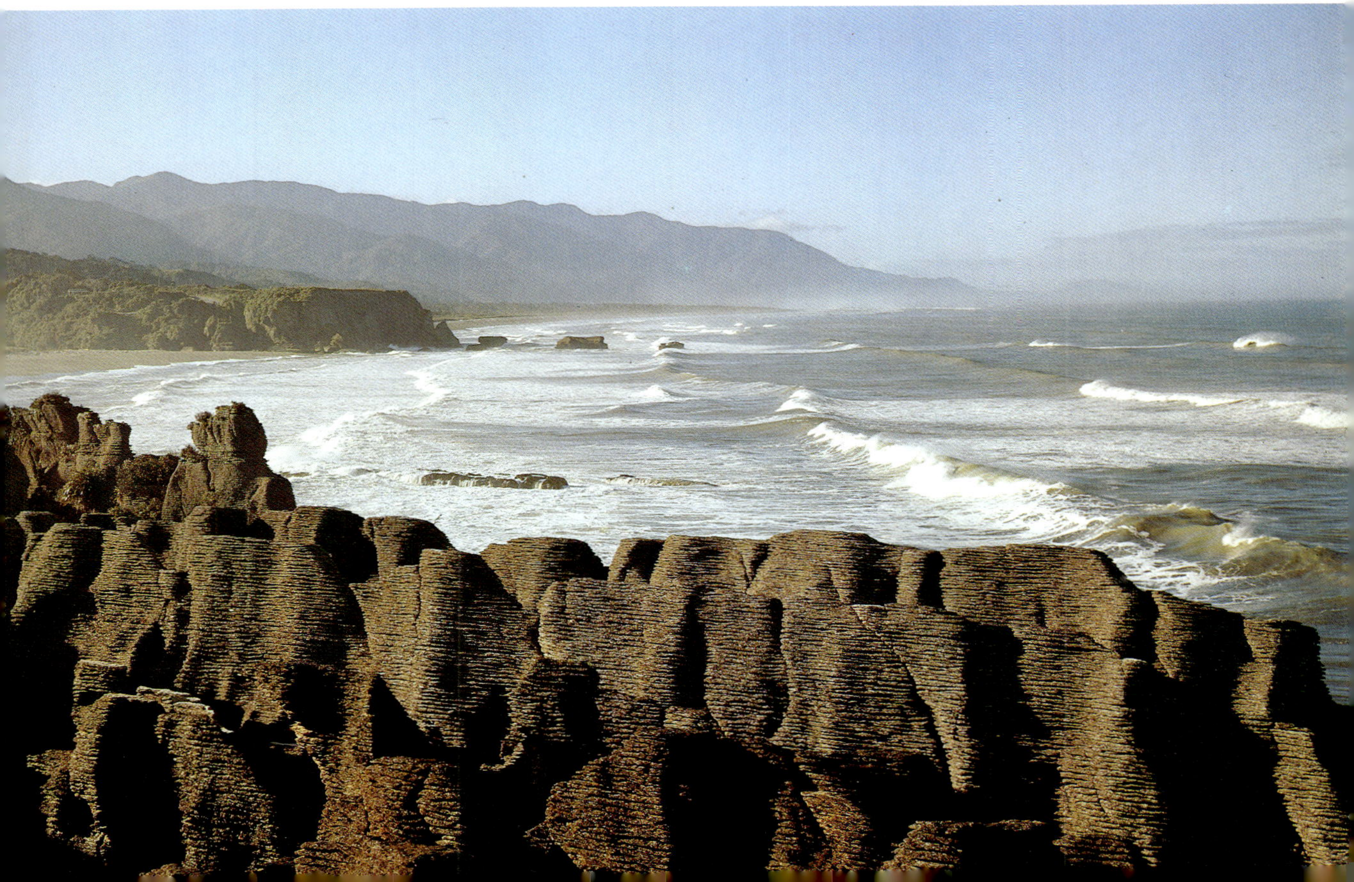

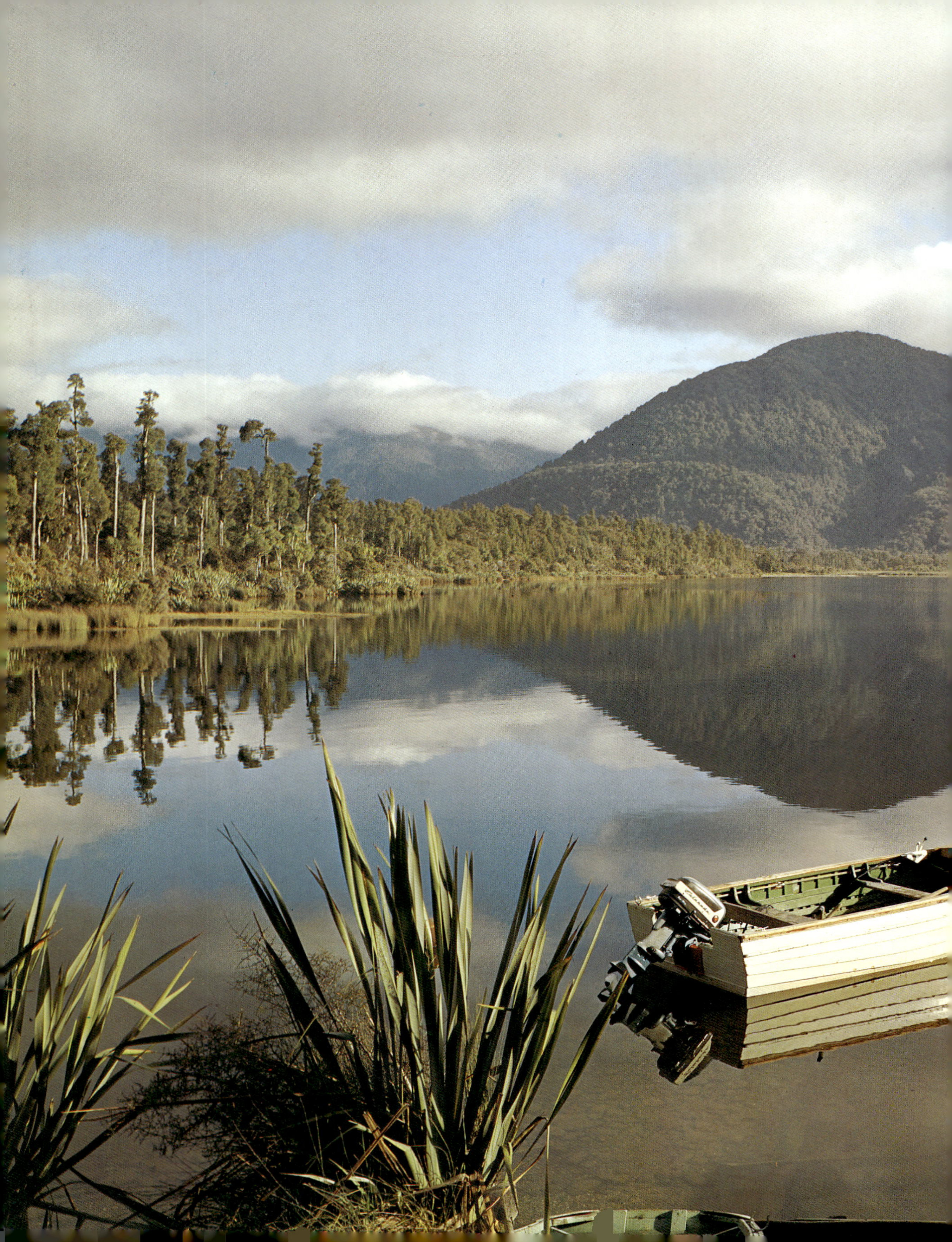

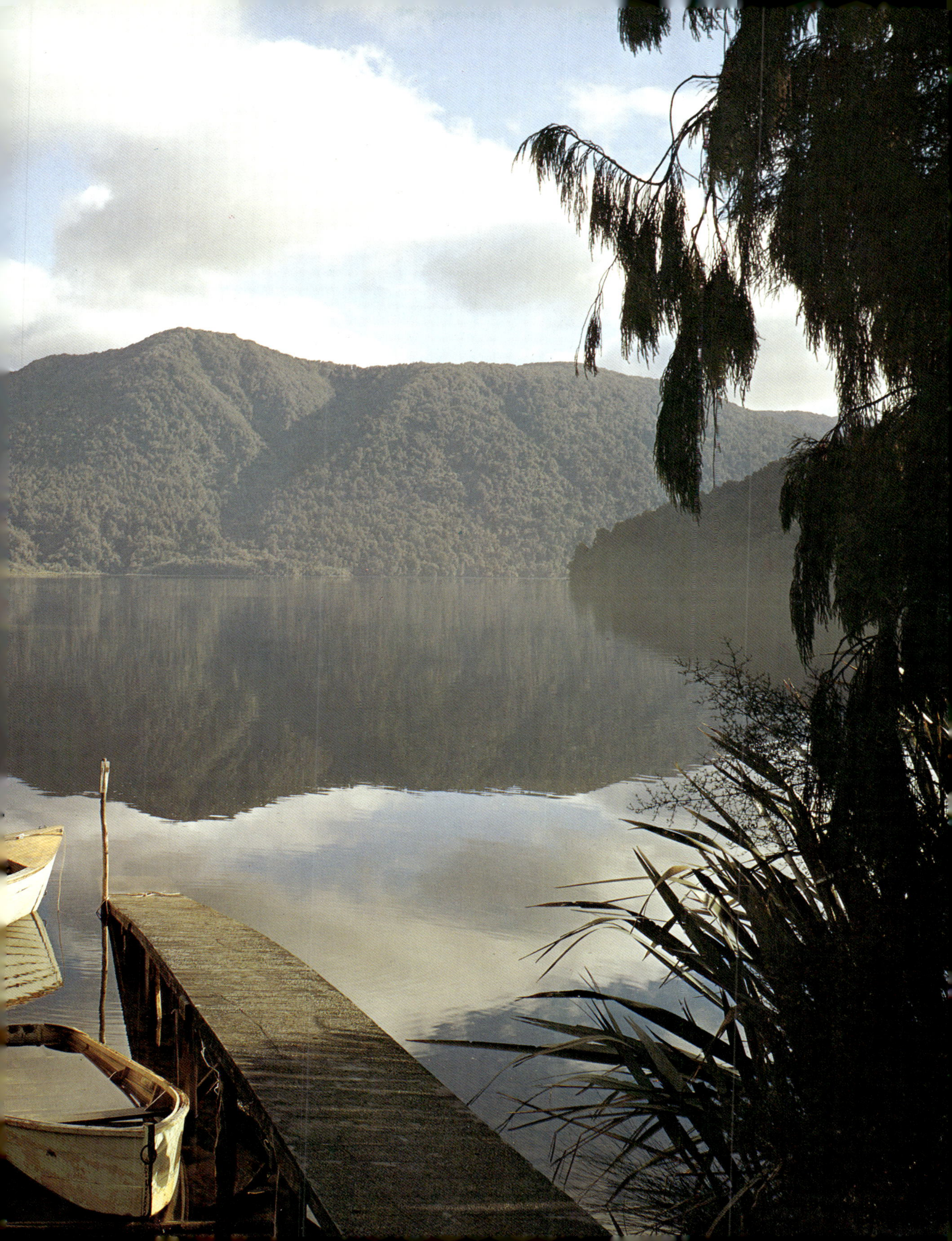

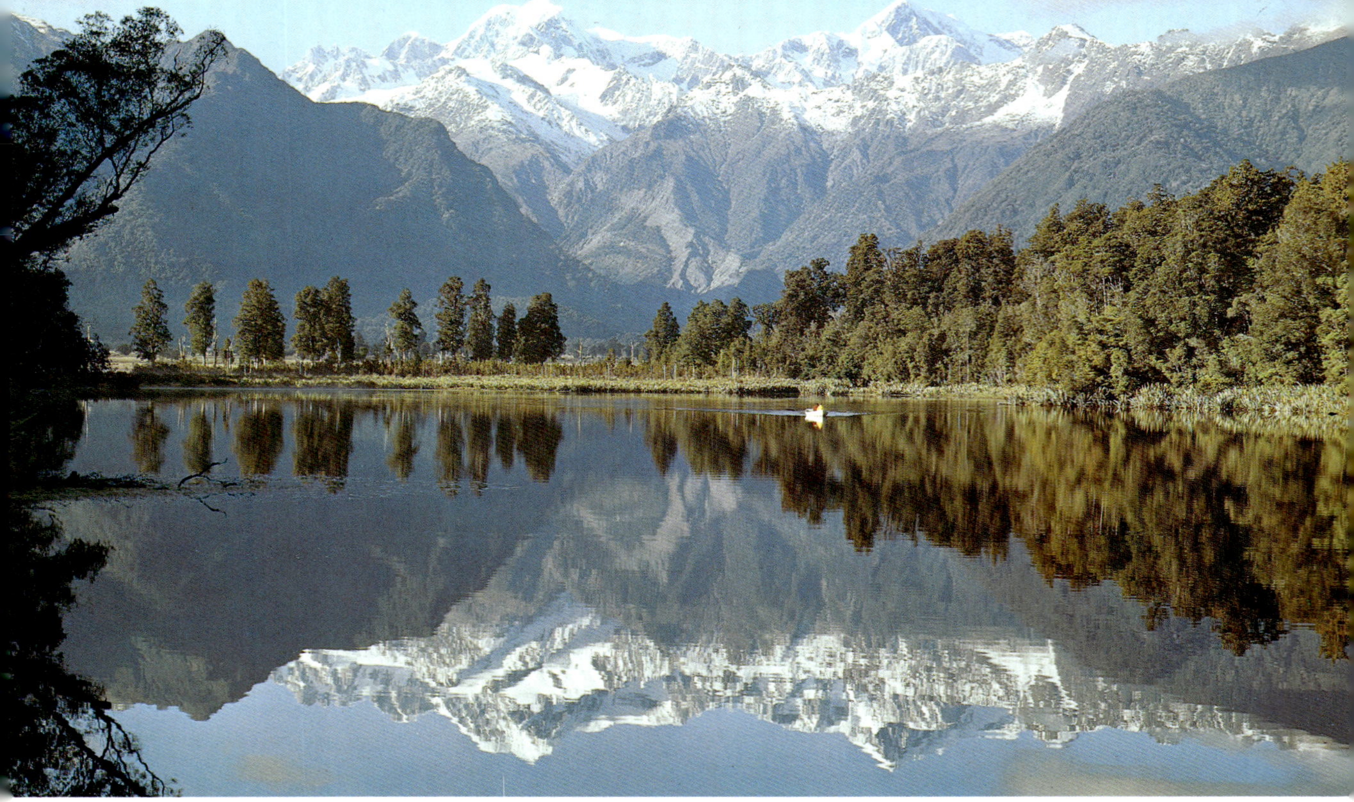

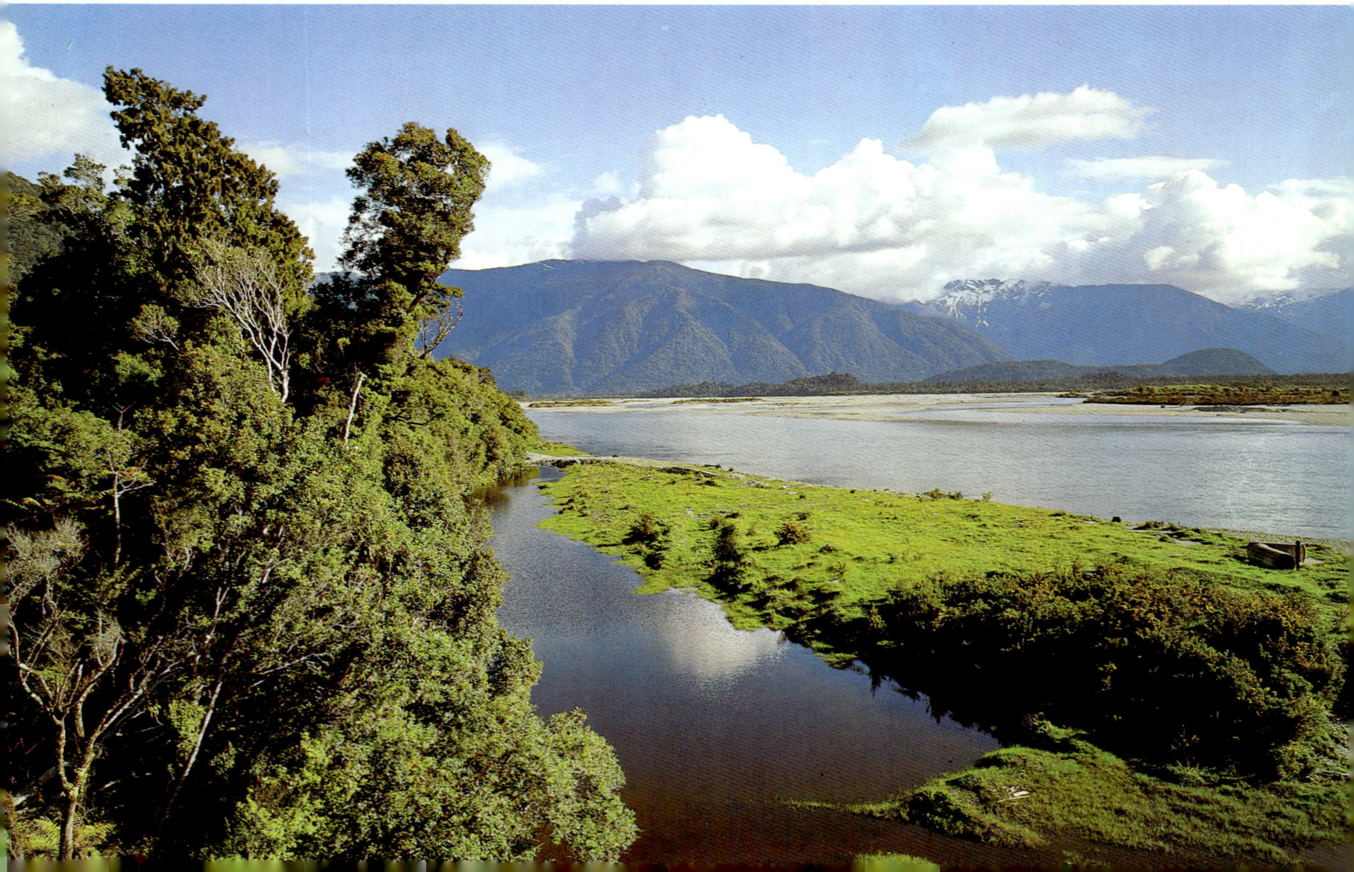

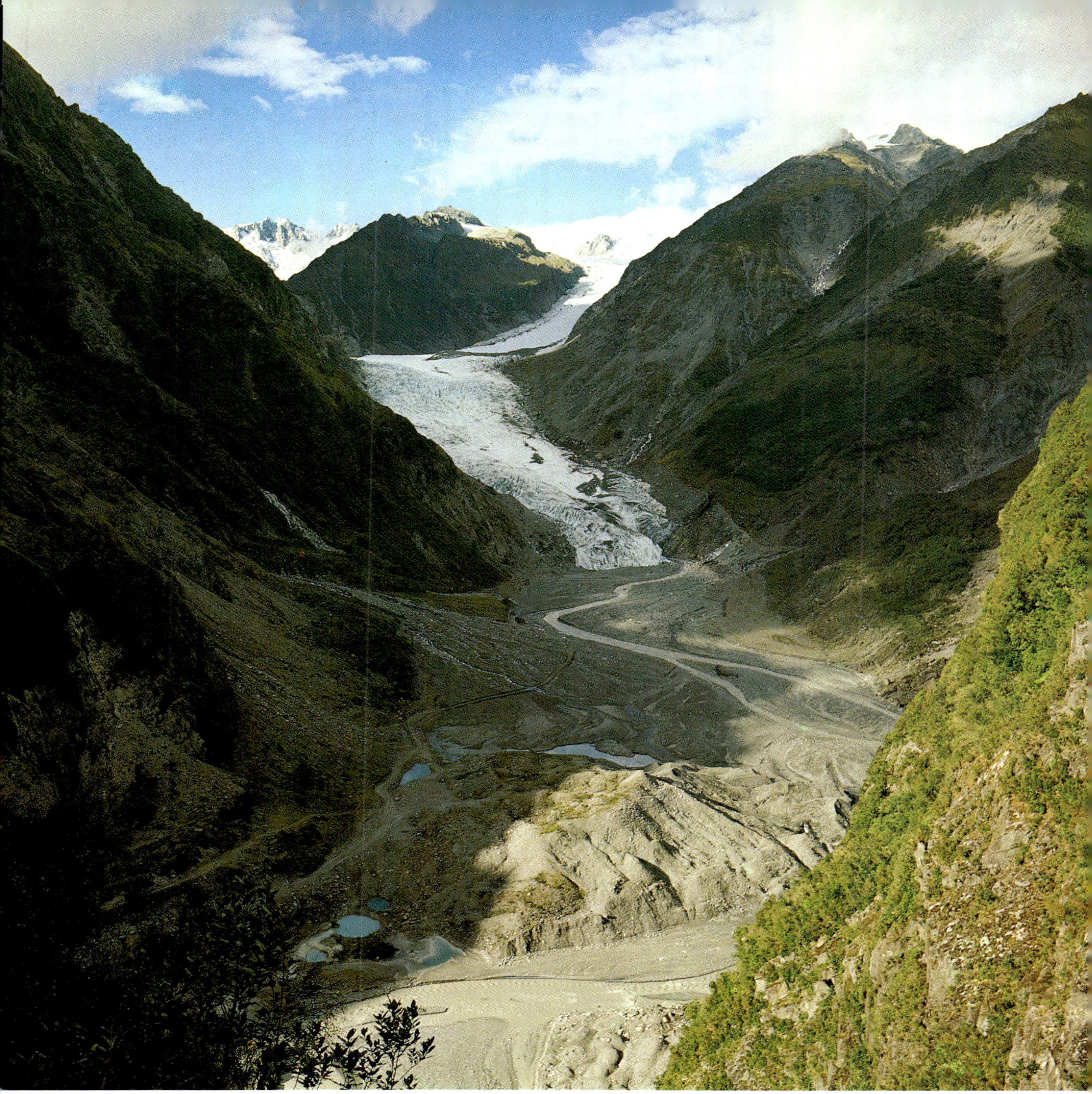

Calm stillness, swift turbulence and slow power are represented in Lake Matheson, (top left), formed by the melting of a huge block of "dead" ice left behind by a receding glacier; the Haast River, (bottom left), which rushes down from the mountains to spread across a broad valley on its way to the sea; and the Fox Glacier, (above), 13km long, sliding down inexorably from vast snowfields beneath 3,000m peaks.

The name of Lake Paringa, (previous page) means "Flowing Tide," alluding to its habit in flood times of flowing with the current of its feeding and draining streams.

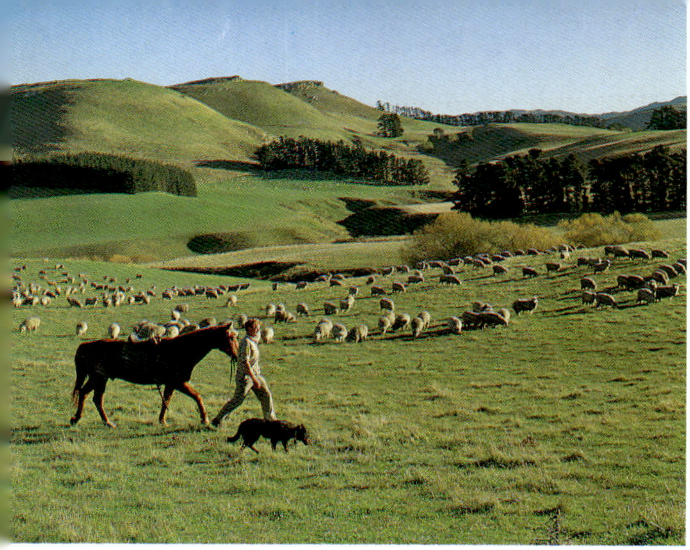

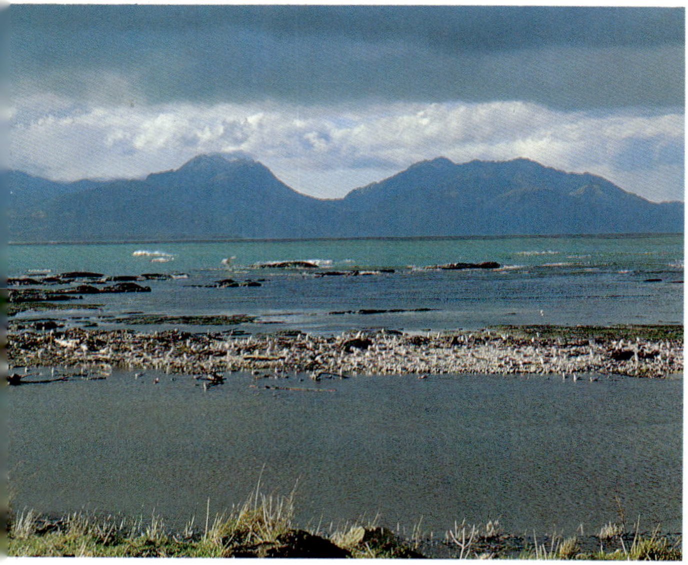

The Kaikoura coast, (above), is famous for the succulence of its crayfish and the height of its mountains that rear 2,800m above the bay. The gentle, rolling, North Canterbury hills about Waikari, (above, top), are renowned for their rich pastures. Banks Peninsula, thrusting out from the plains and rising over 500m, is notable for its two great, deep-water, volcanic crater harbours, Lyttelton, the main commercial port, and Akaroa (right), idyllic holiday settlement which was once a French colony.

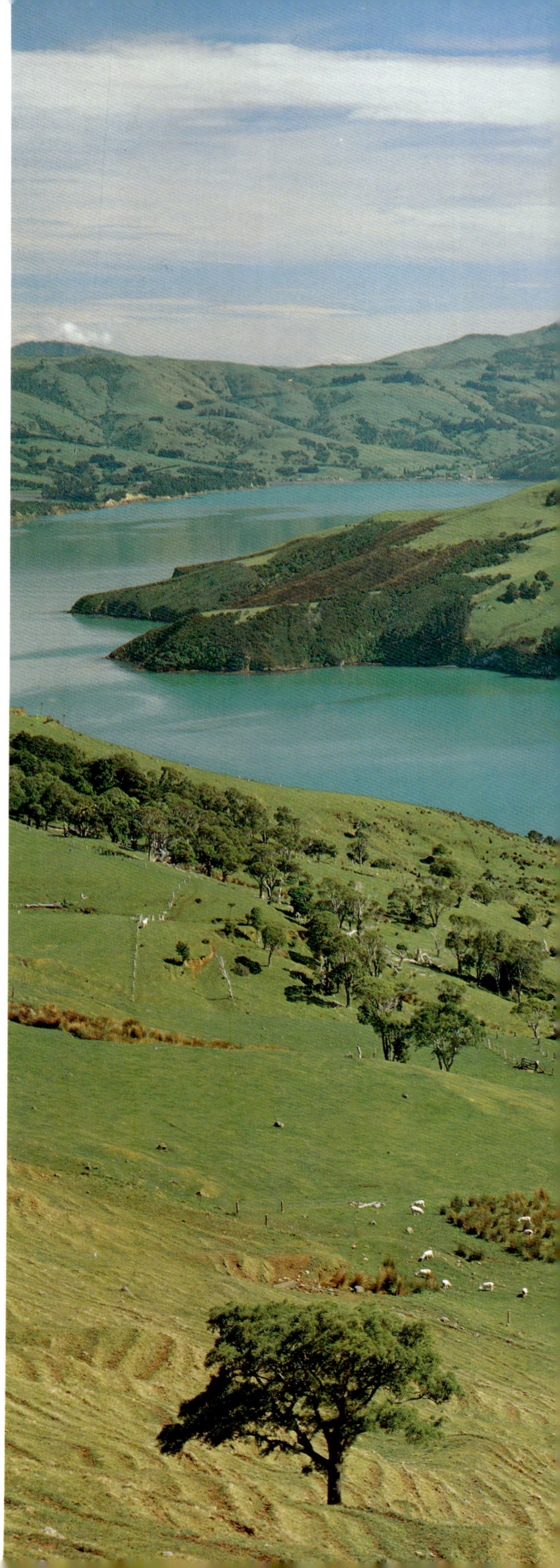

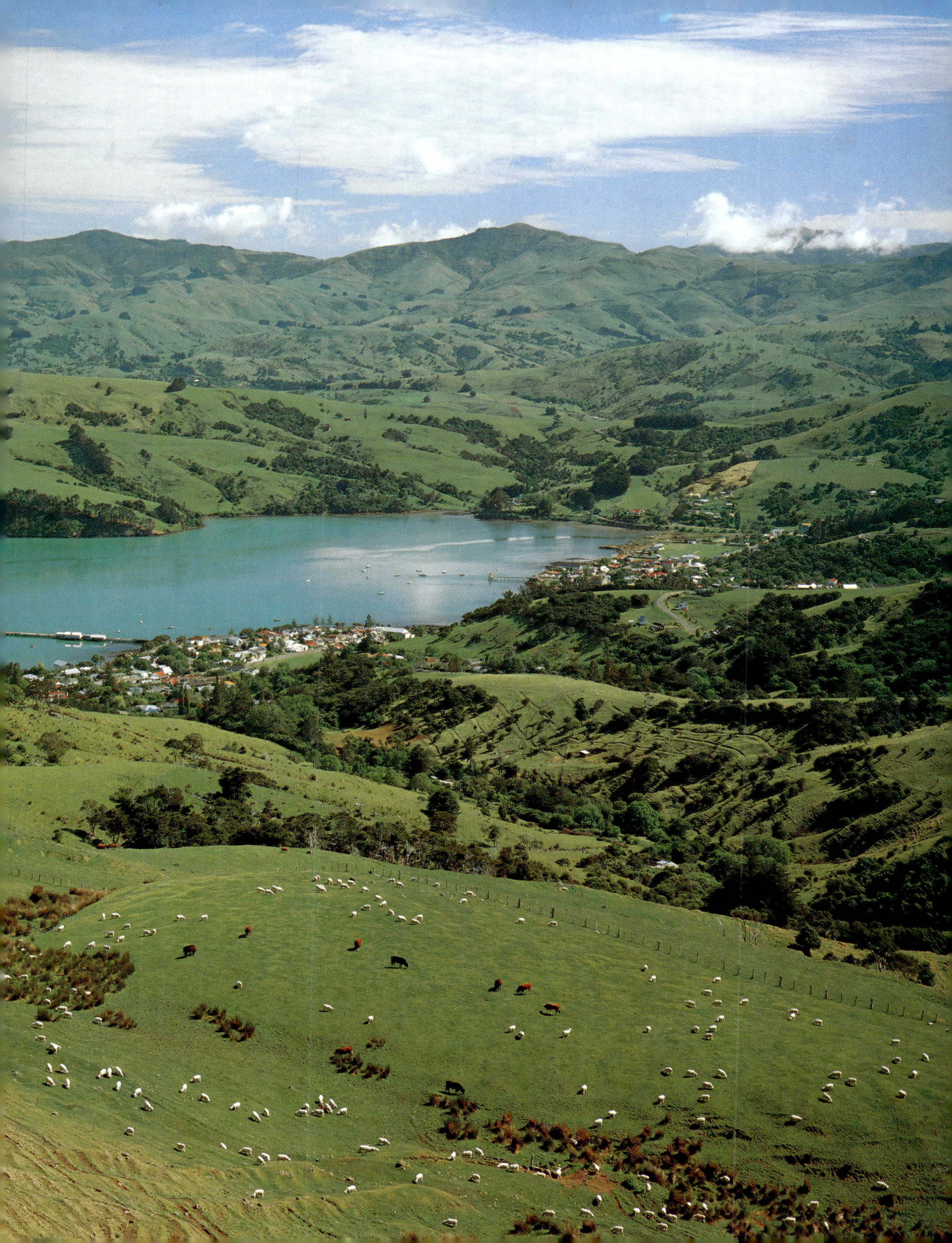

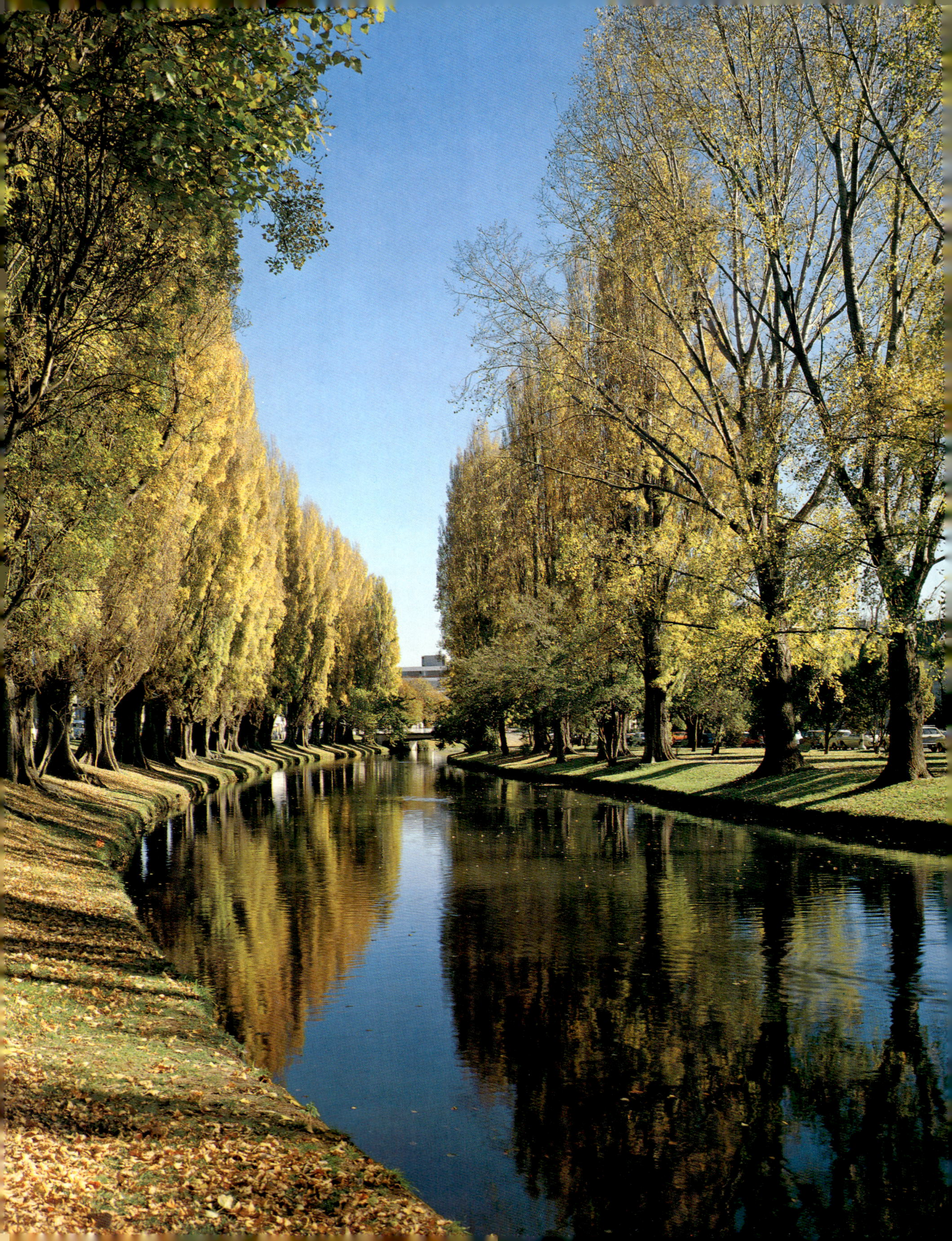

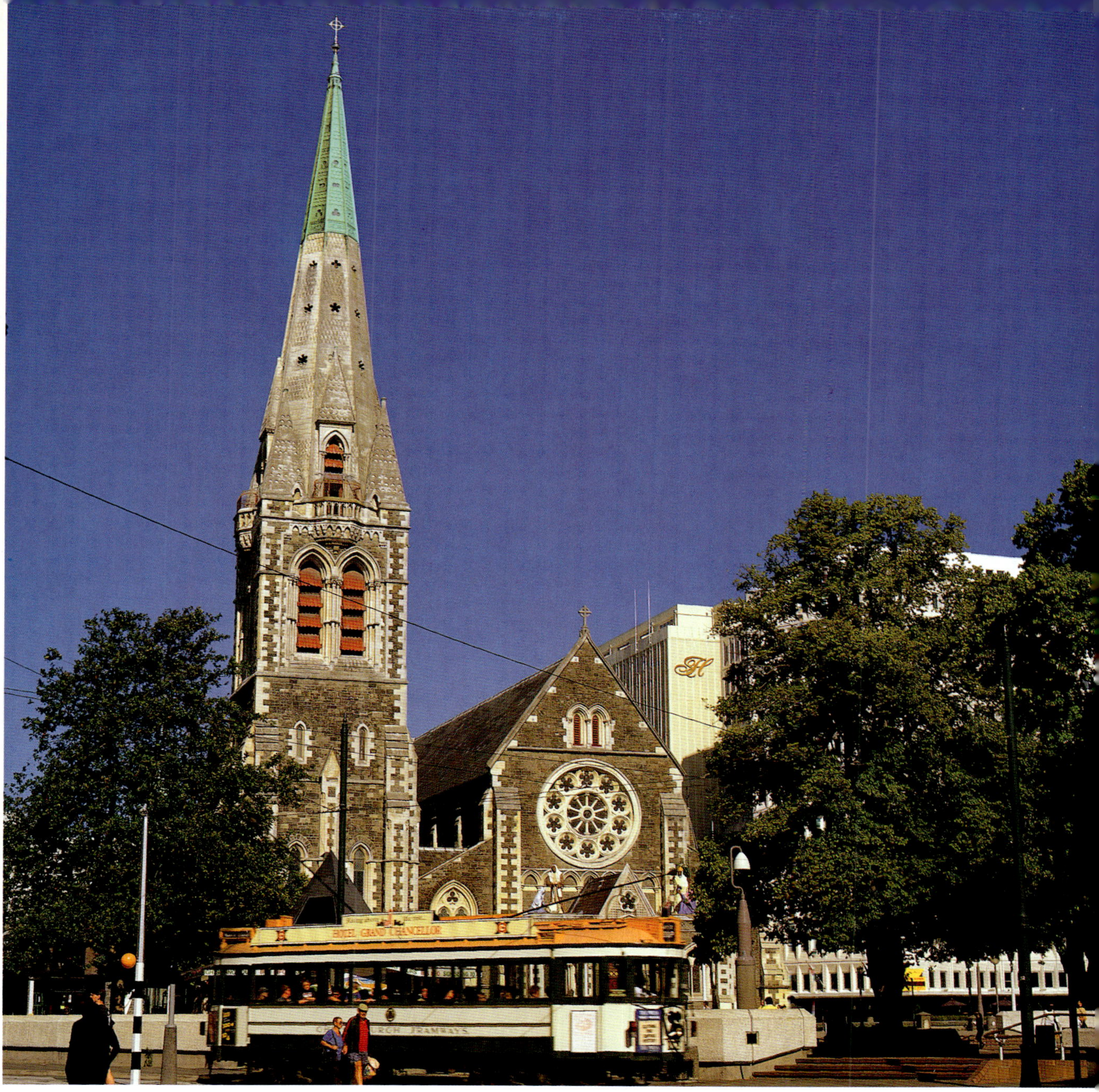

Christchurch's Anglican Cathedral (above), with its 64m spire, still commands the tiled plaza of Cathedral Square, where it has stood for over 100 years. In front of the cathedral is one of the city's famous trams. The Avon River (left) adds to Christchurch's charm and English character. Once navigated by shallow-draft vessels carrying freight and sightseers, the river still carries children in canoes and tourists in punts along its tree-lined reaches.

The South Island's chief glory is its upland basins such as the Mackenzie Country, with mountain-girt lakes including Pukaki, (right), (at the very foot of Mount Cook, 3,664m); and the lovely little Lake Alexandrina, (right, lower), whose Maori name was Te Waiatekamoana, "The Water of the Crested Grebe;" and the high Alps, with the great, eternal snowfields like the neve beneath Mt. Cook's western face, (below), feeding the Fox Glacier.

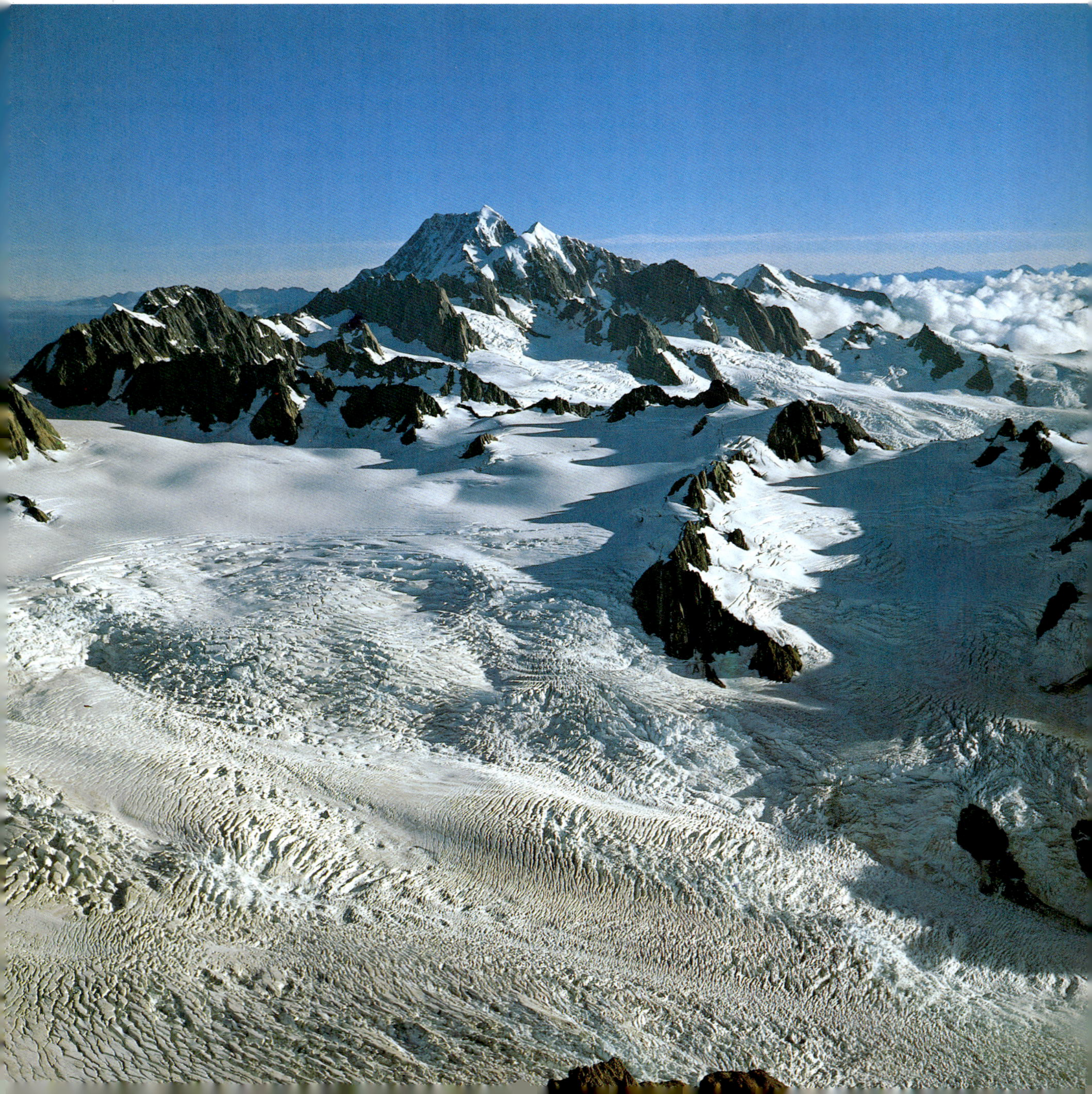

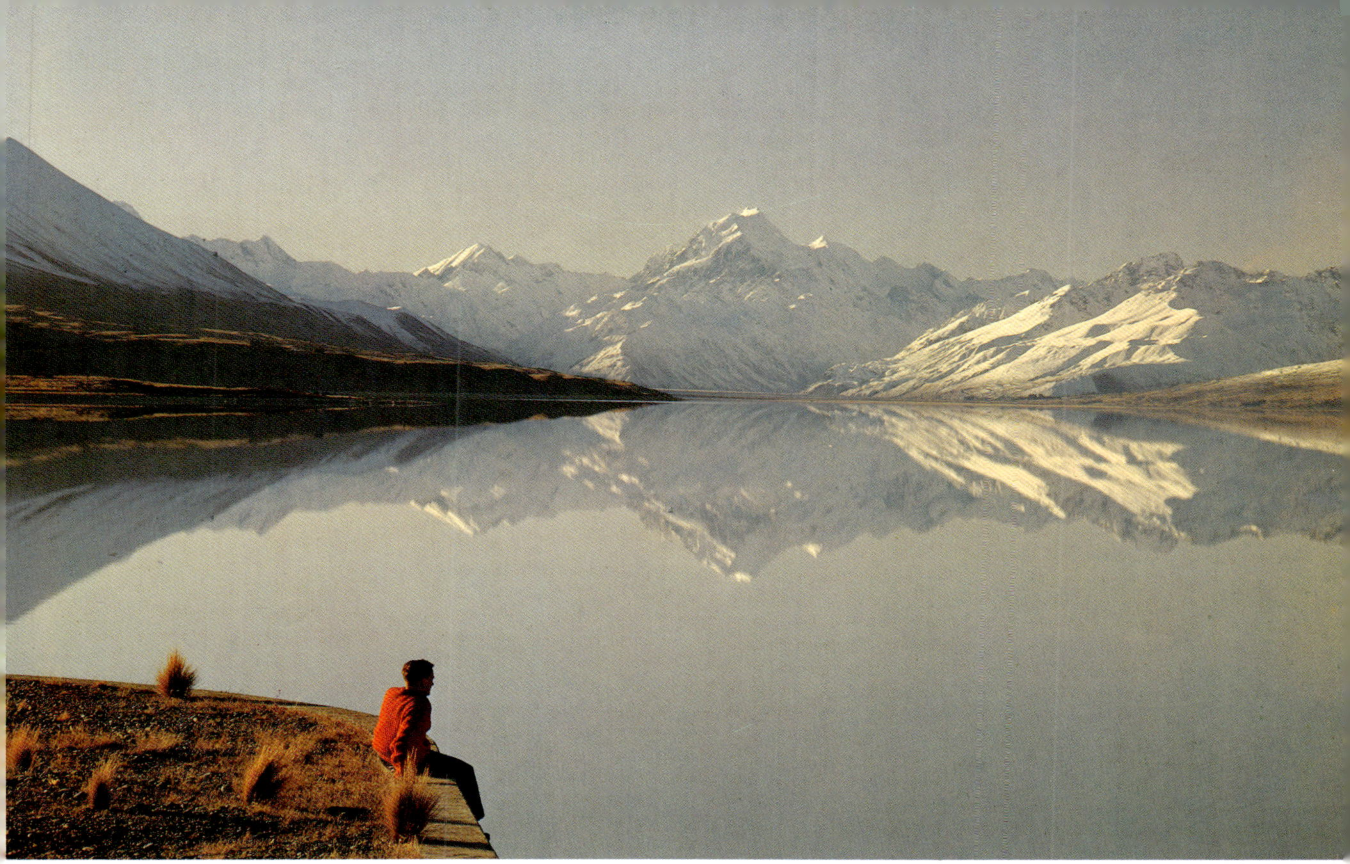

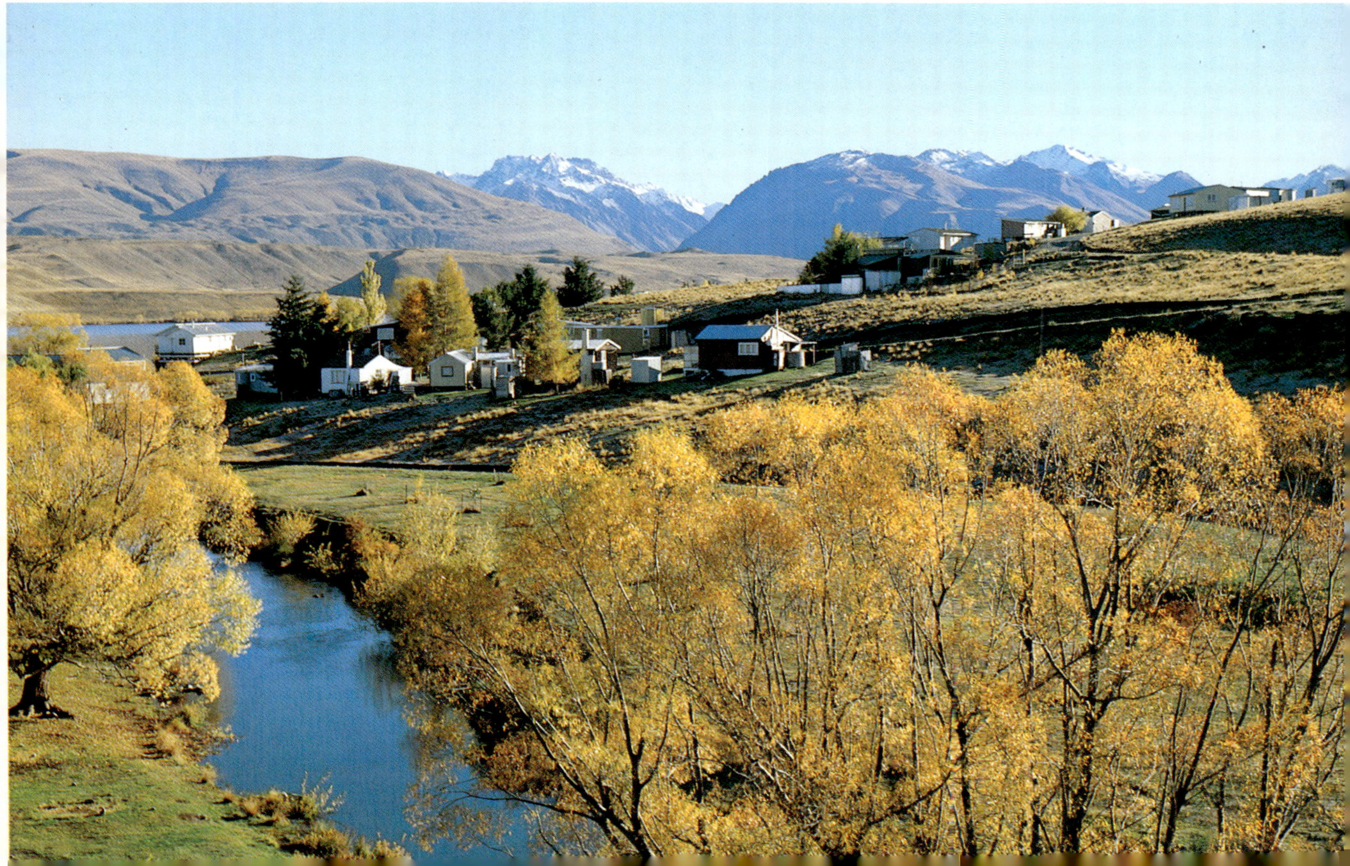

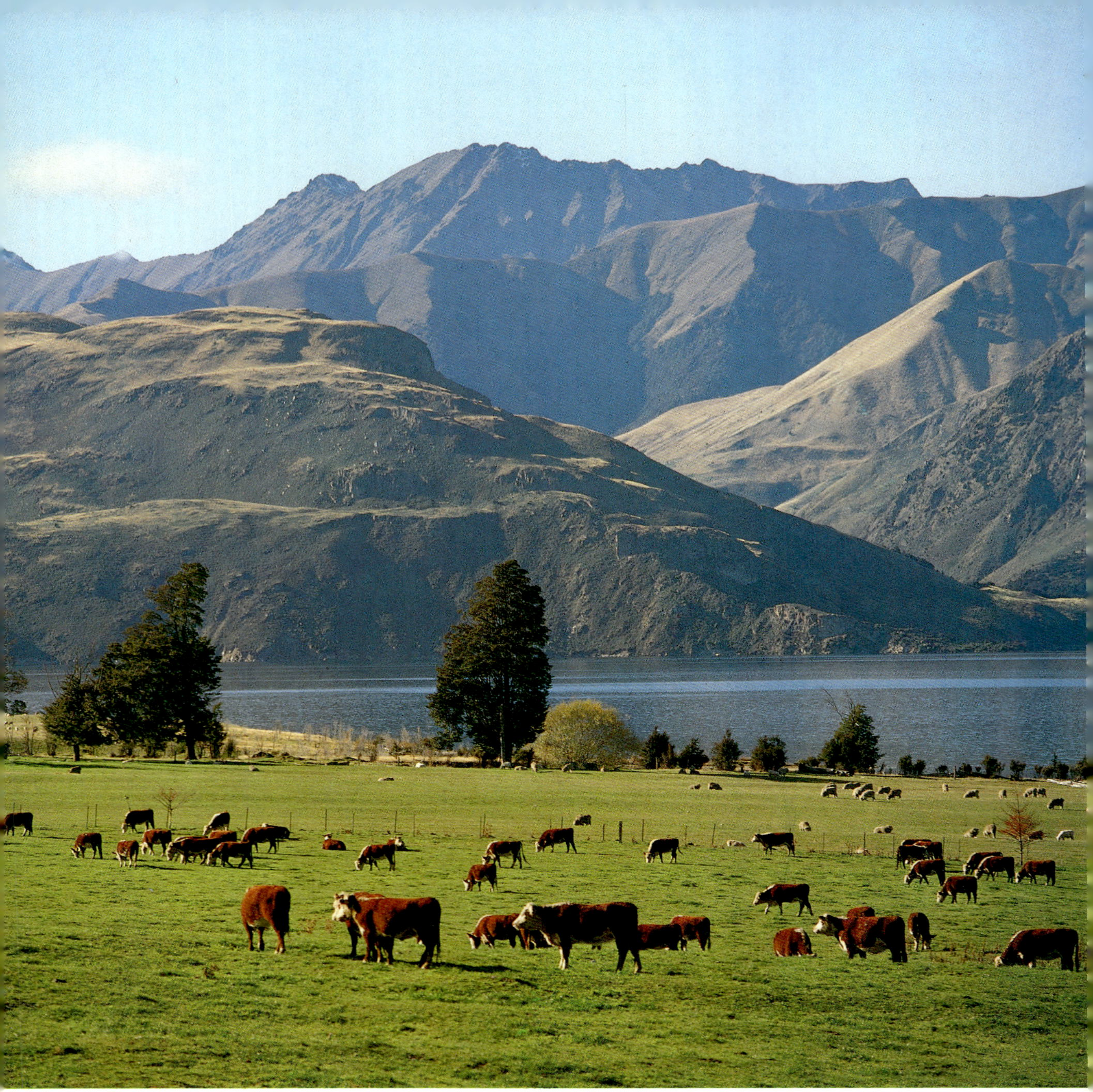

Lake Hawea, (above), in the 22 miles long by 5 miles wide bed of an ancient glacier, is bordered by gently sloping land which traps the sun, and used to grow bumper crops of wheat. Now it grazes sheep and Hereford cattle. Nearby Lake Wanaka, (right), over 300m deep and island-dotted, with deeply indented shoreline, covers some 75 square miles. Lake Tekapo, (overleaf), in the Mackenzie Country, lies more than 426m higher than Wanaka or Hawea, and, like Hawea, occupies the bed of an ancient glacier, covering some 32 square miles.

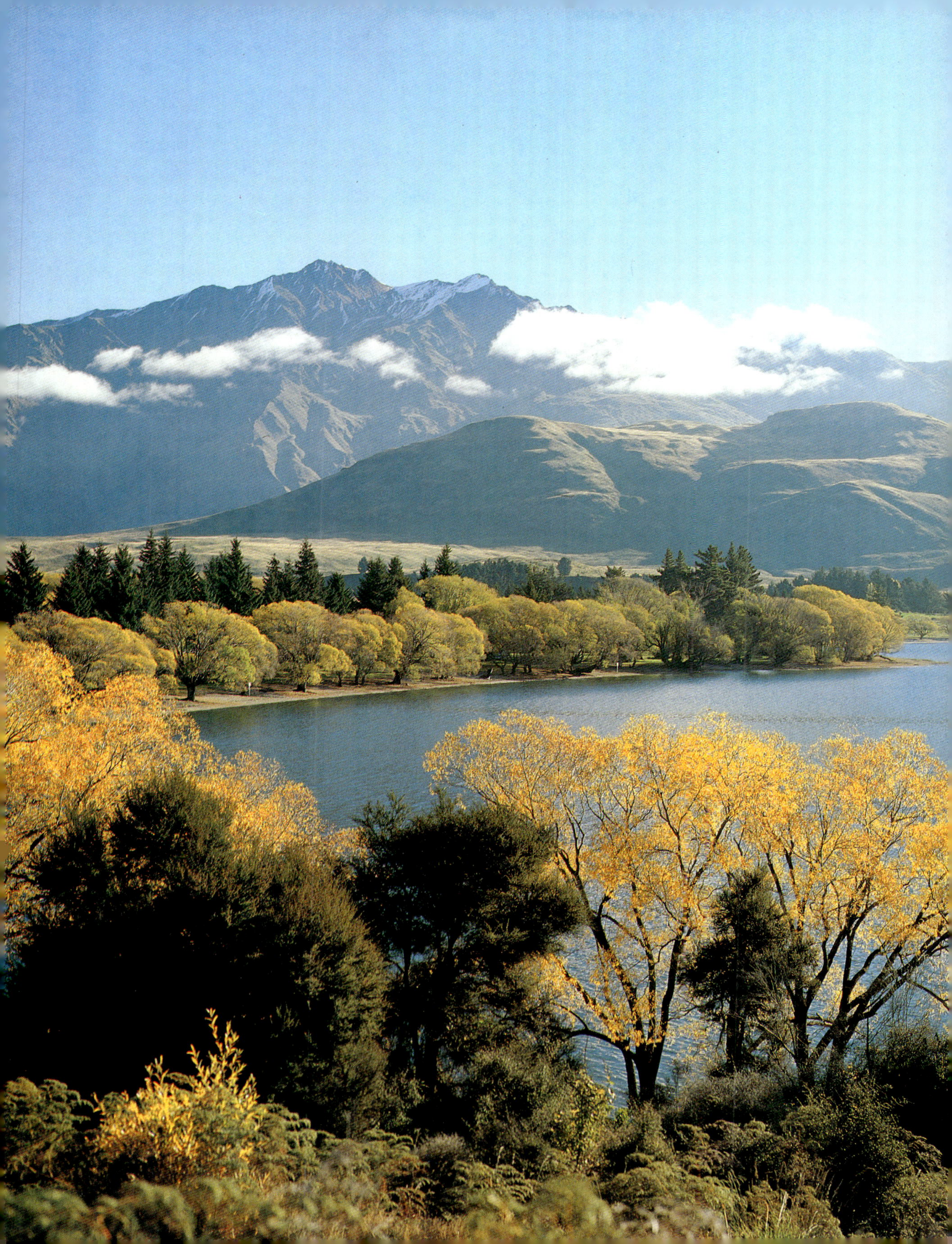

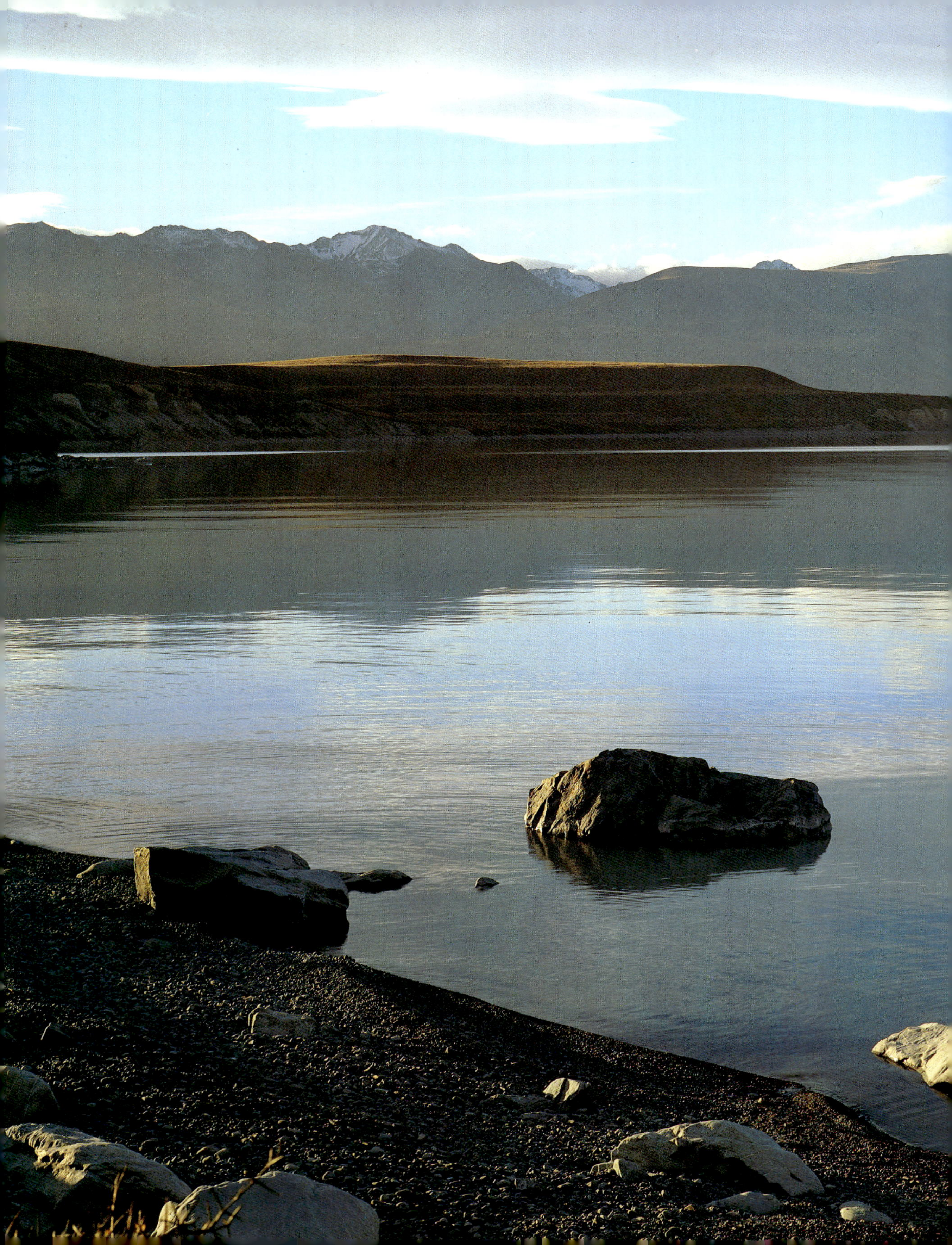

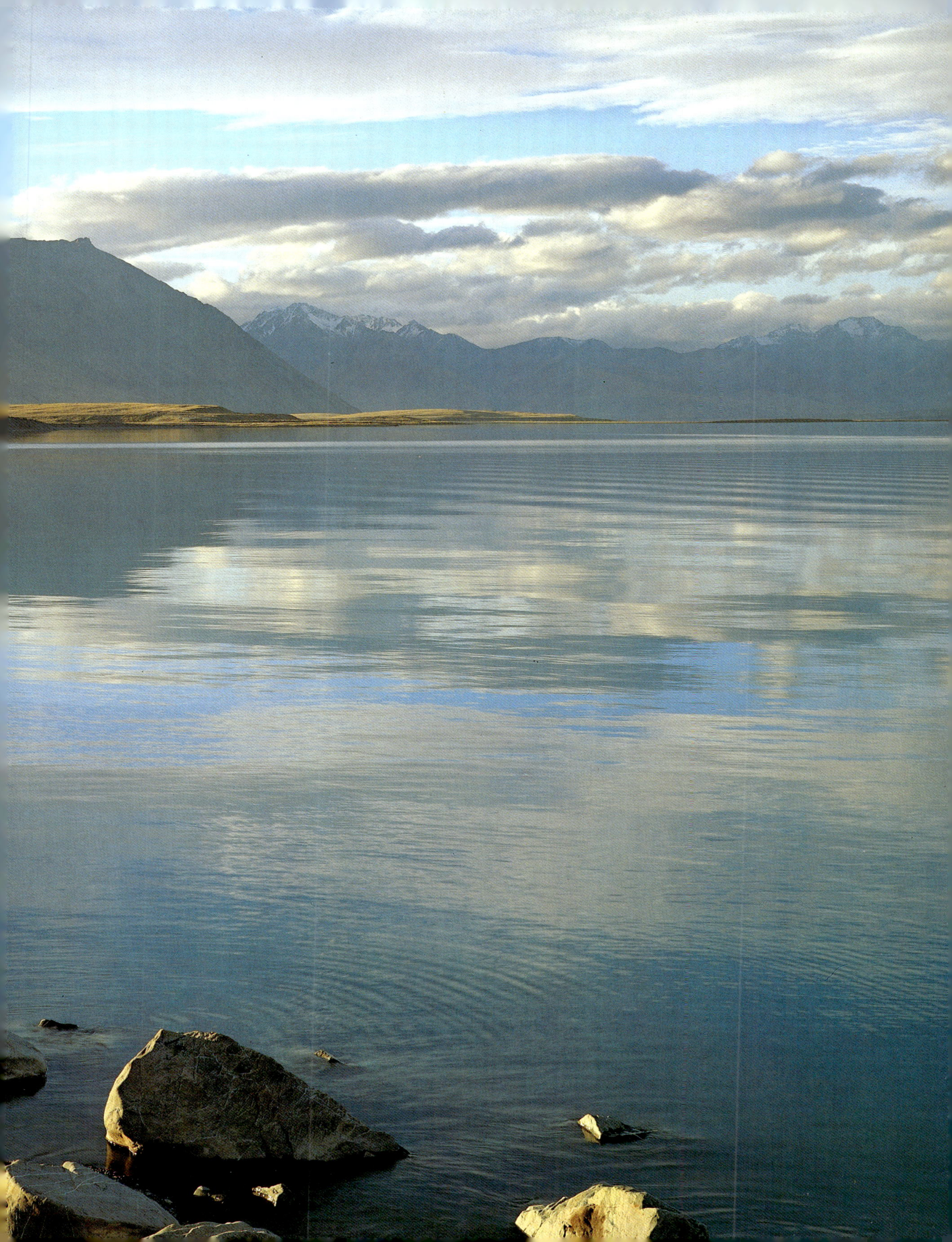

The Lake Wakatipu district abounds in surprises — the lovely Lake Hayes, (right), in scenes of pastoral gentleness and famous for its trout, (limit bag 20 fish!), contrasting with Queenstown, (right, bottom), set in the alpine grandeur of mountain-walled Lake Wakatipu itself, 52 miles long and up to 3 miles wide, its altitude 309m, its bottom 89m below sea level; and the Routeburn Track, (below), a three-day walk from the top of Lake Wakatipu to the Hollyford Valley, over country which ranges from bare, windswept uplands, to dense forest and pasture-like river flats such as these under Mount Homus.

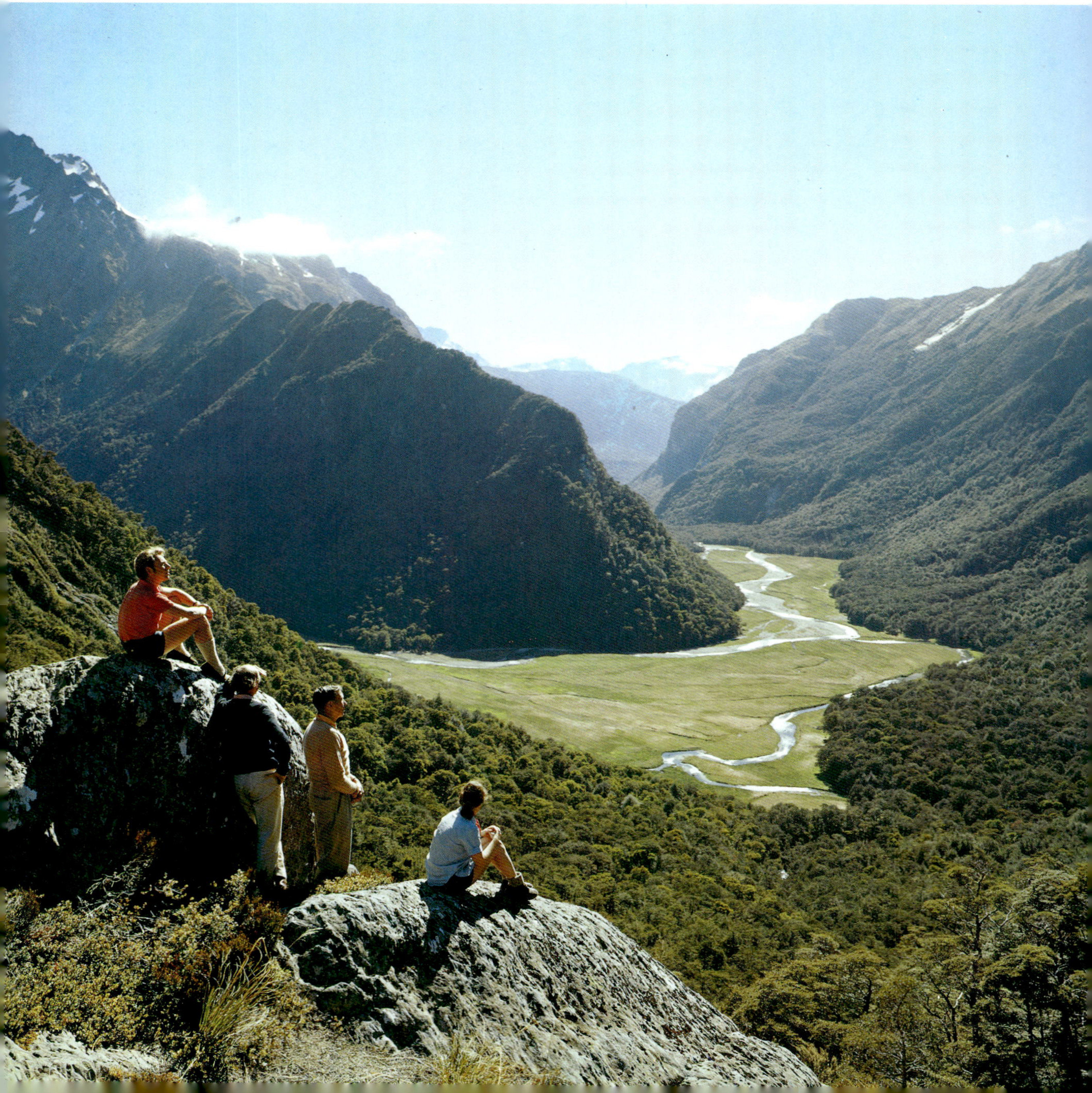

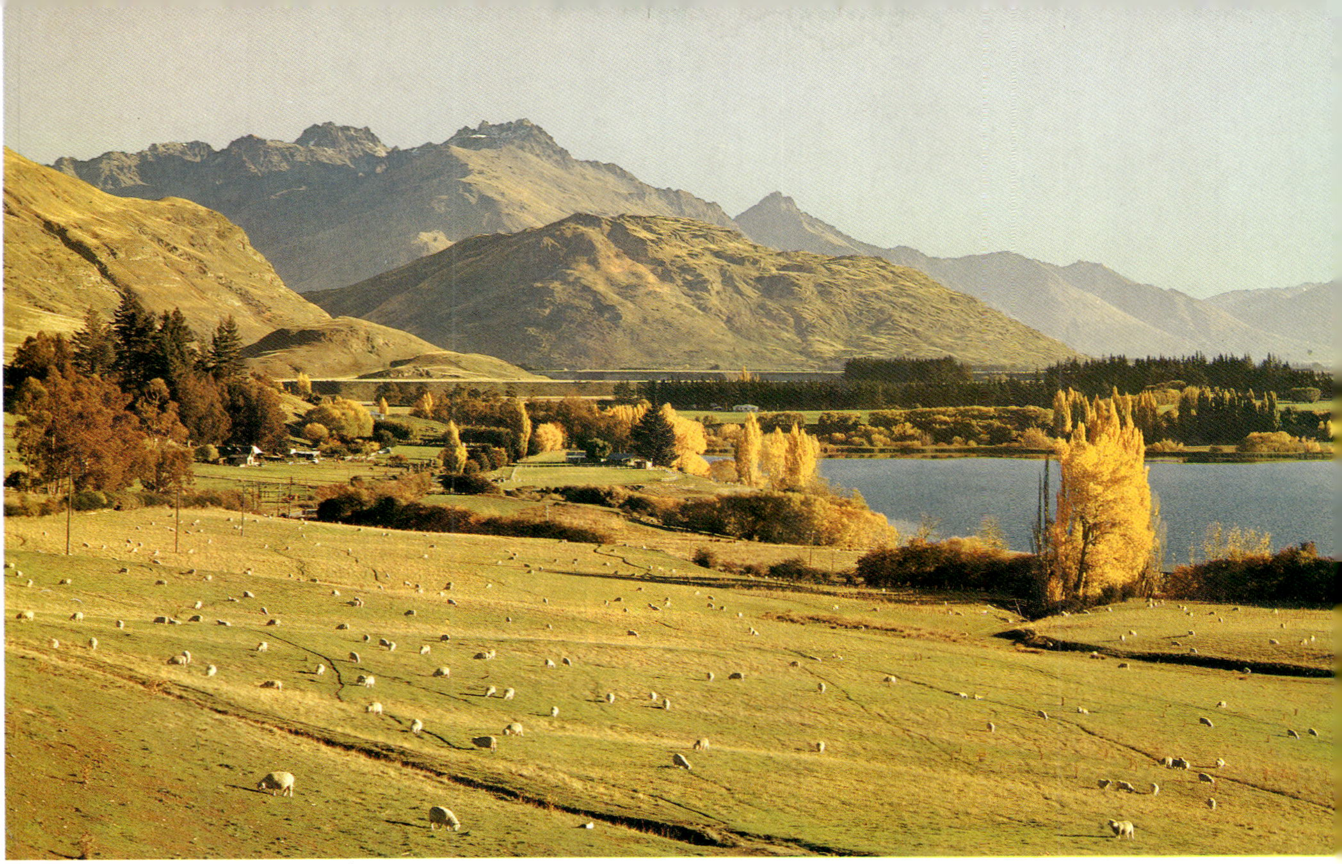

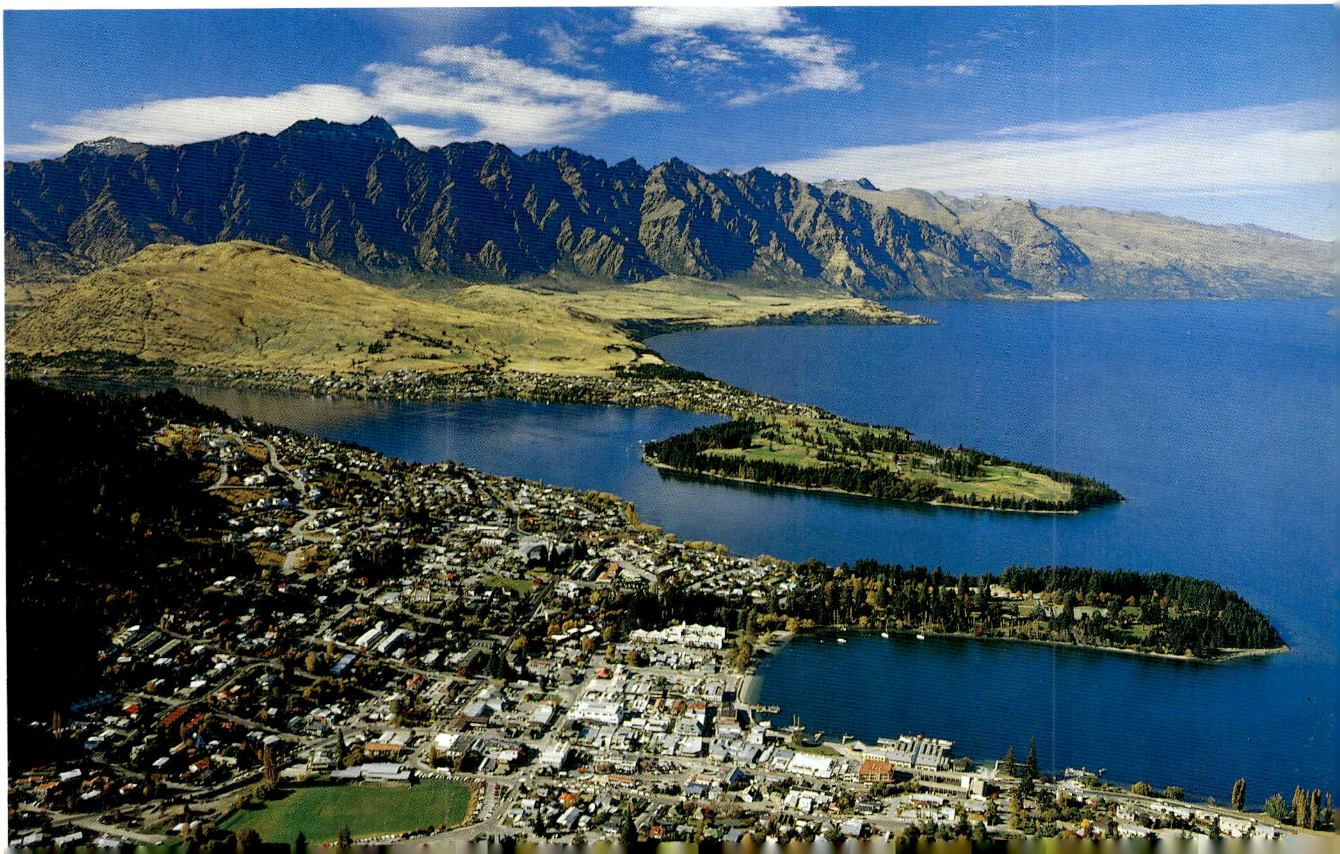

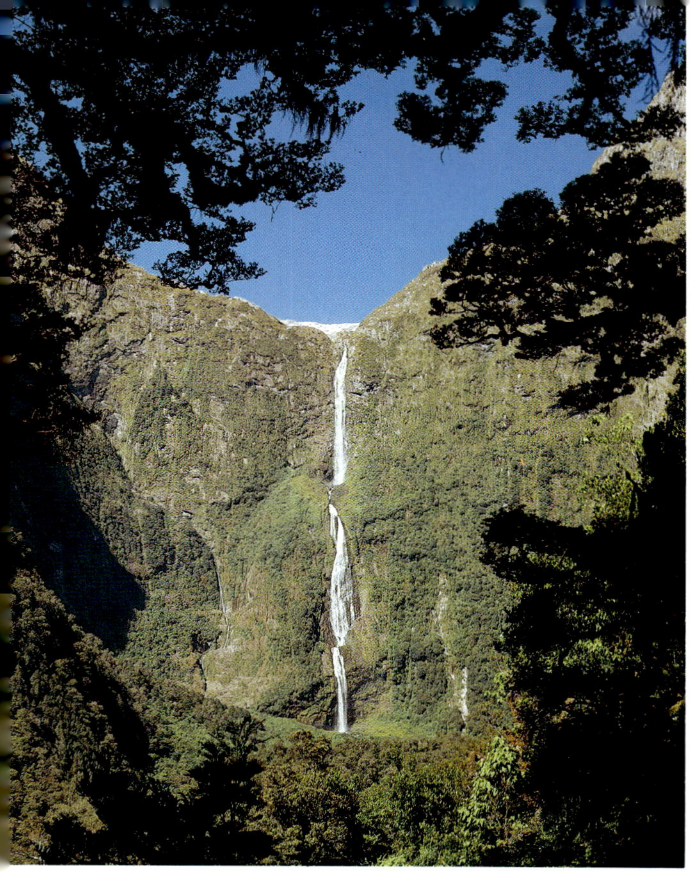

The Sutherland Falls, (above), third highest in the world, plunging down from the jug-like lip of Lake Quill, 580m in three giant leaps, form one of the many spectacular sights along the famous Milford Track, a three-day walk from the head of Lake Te Anau to Milford Sound, where mountains like the famed Mitre Peak, (right), rise sheer for over 1,500m from the water.

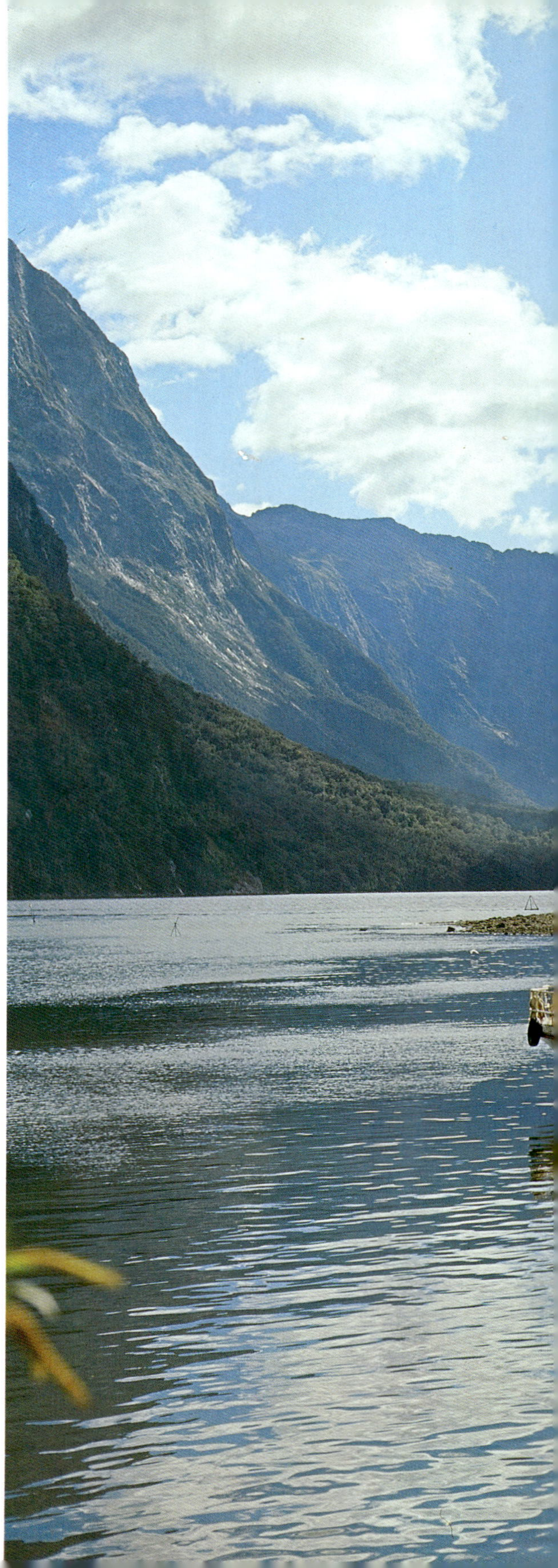

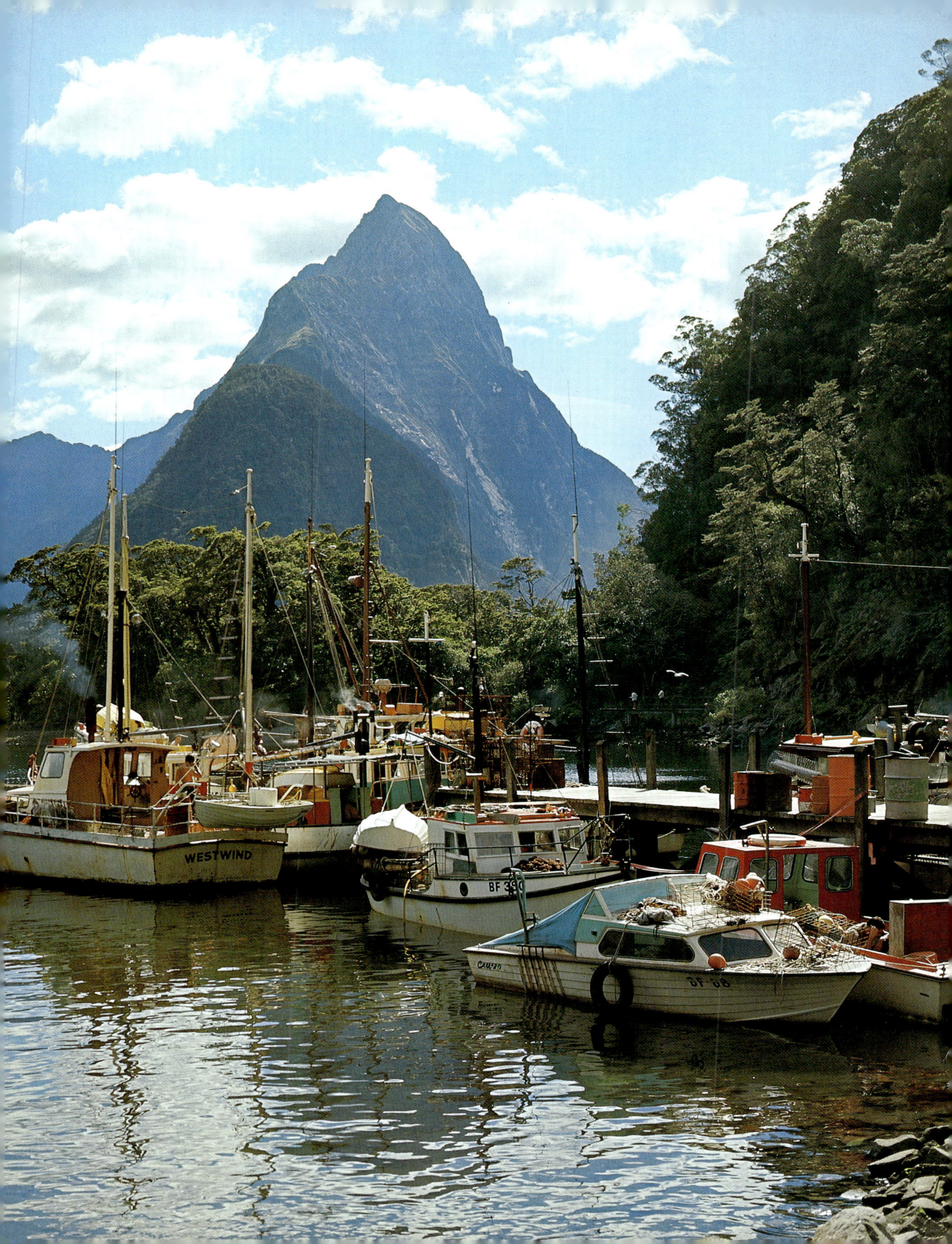
WESTWIND

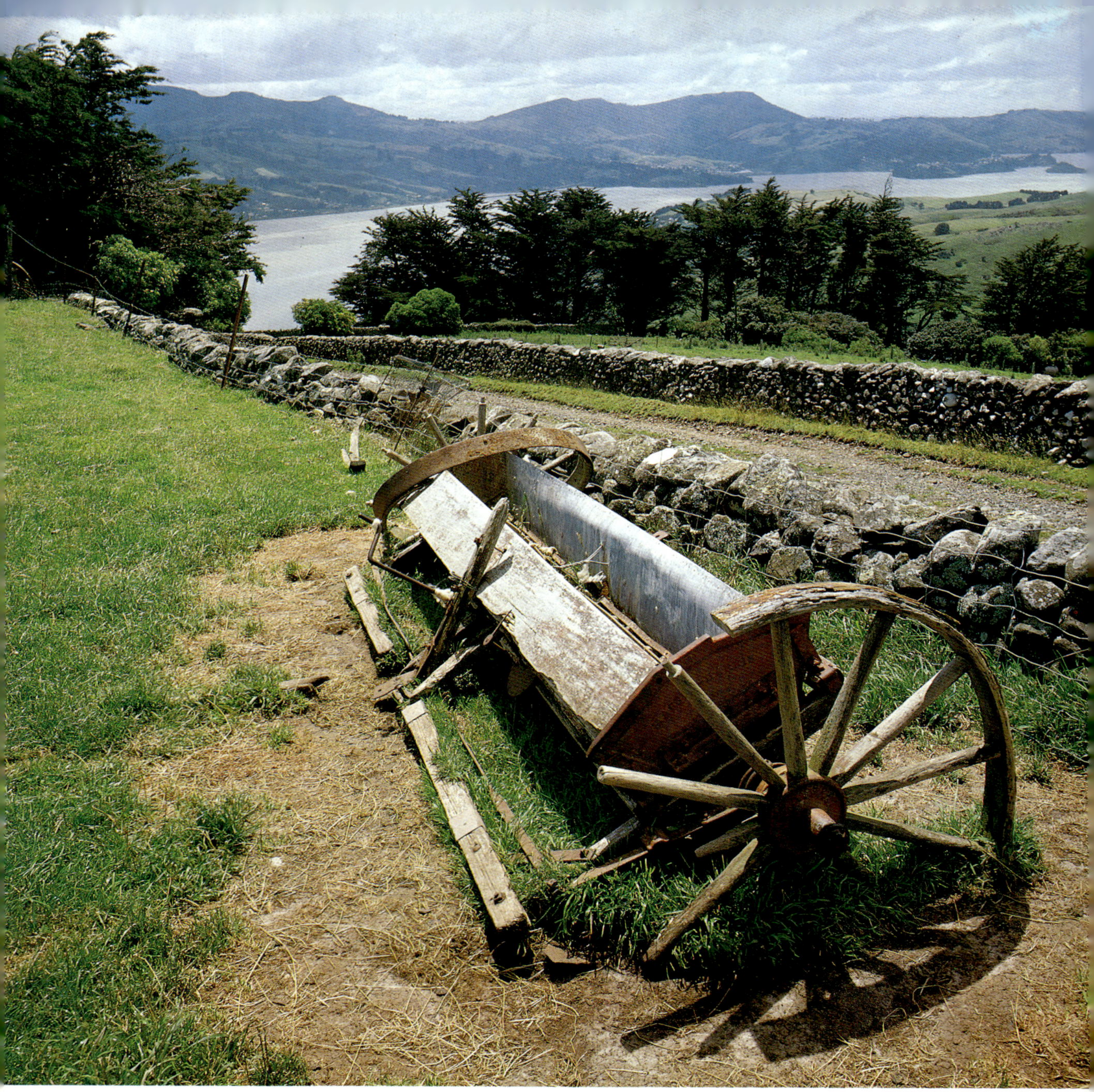

The Scottish settlers on Otago Peninsula soon transformed a wild and rocky landscape into a network of neat crofts dividing their fields with drystone walls, (above), while the more urban-minded settlers built the town of Dunedin, (right, above), which grew wealthy from the Otago Goldrush in the 1860's-70's, and was for long the largest, best appointed city in New Zealand. Farthest south was the gold- and tin-mining settlement at Pegasus Bay, now abandoned, on Stewart Island — behind which tower Gog and Magog, (right, below), the rugged Fraser Peaks on the southern extremity of the island.

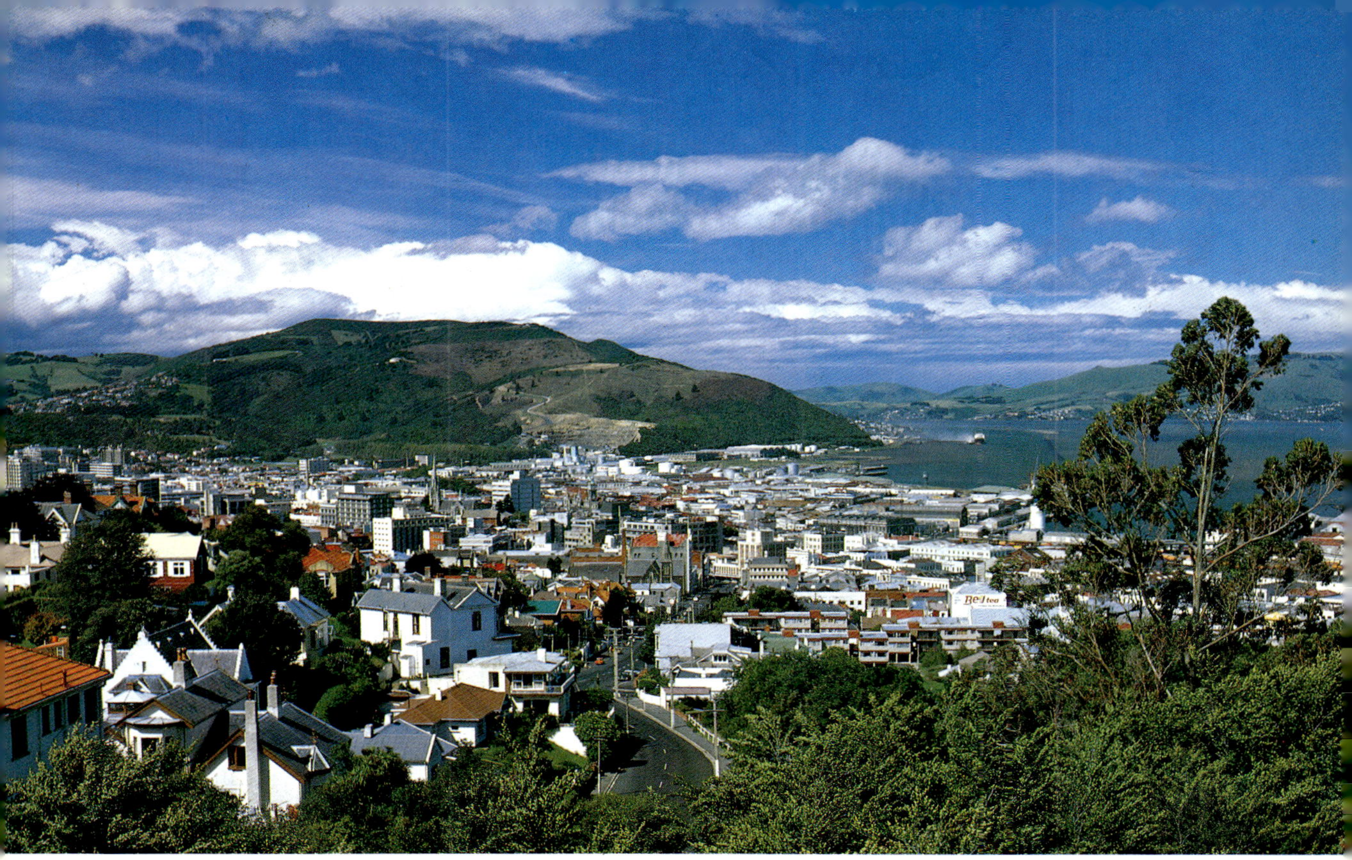

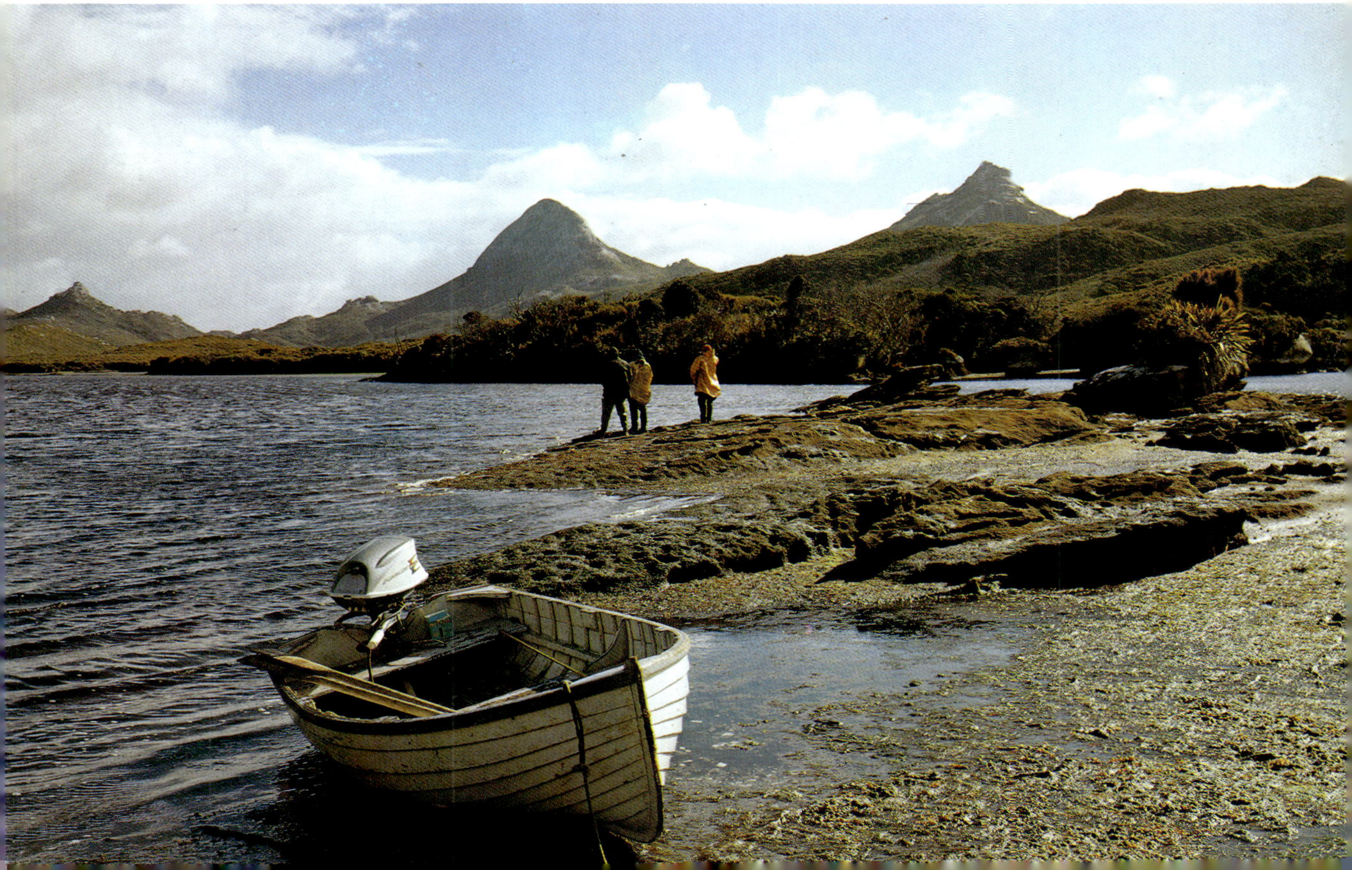

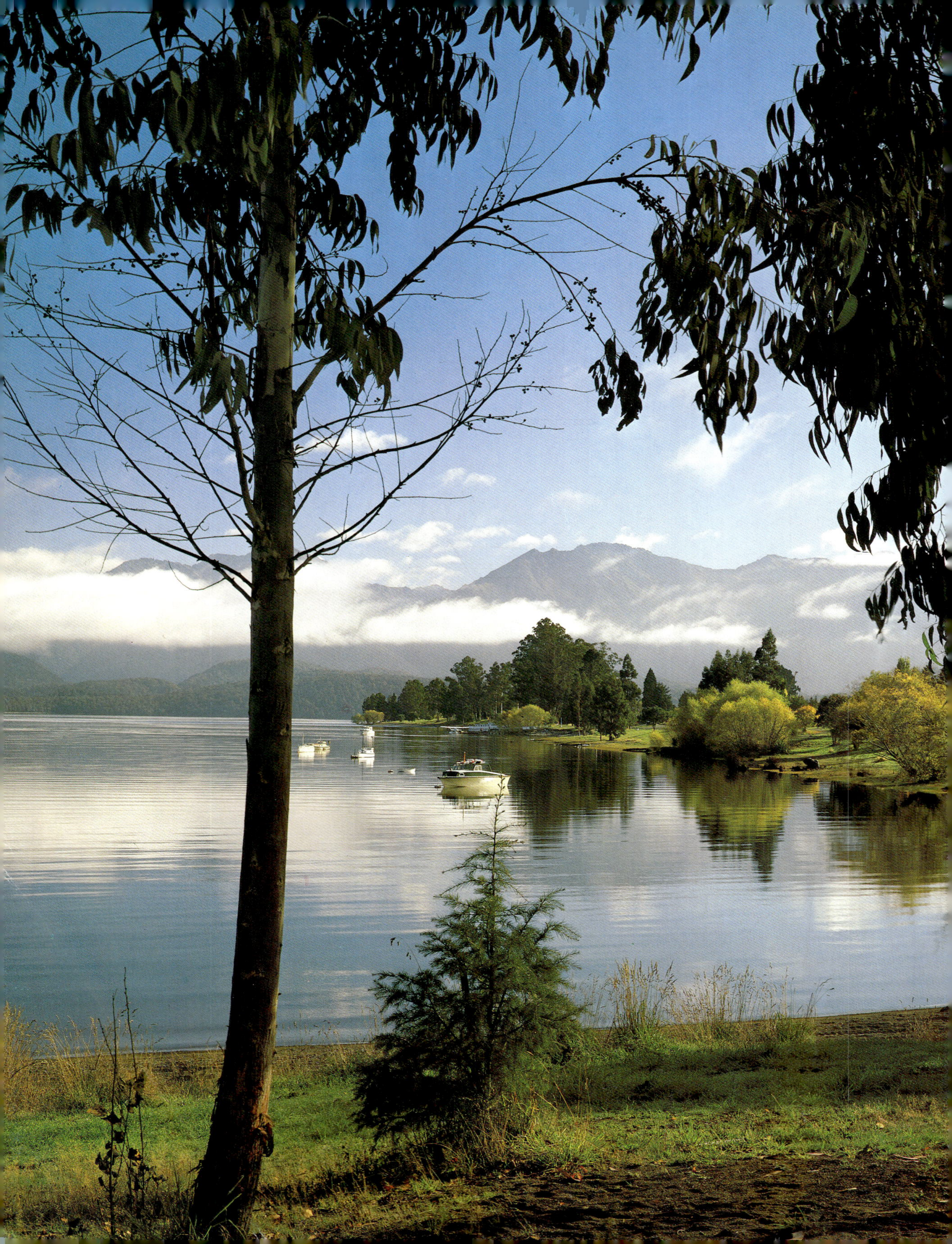